## DATE DUE

# My First Seven Years
## (plus a few more)

Selected Works by Dario Fo

*Archangels Don't Play Pinball*

*Mistero Buffo*

*Accidental Death of an Anarchist*

*Can't Pay? Won't Pay!*

*The Tale of a Tiger*

*Trumpets and Raspberries*

*Elizabeth: Almost by Chance a Woman*

*The Pope and the Witch*

*A Woman Alone*

*About Face*

*The Tricks of the Trade*

*The Peasants' Bible*

# My First Seven Years

(plus a few more)

*A Memoir*

# DARIO FO

*Translated from Italian*
*by Joseph Farrell*

*Thomas Dunne Books*
*St. Martin's Press*
*New York*

THOMAS DUNNE BOOKS.
An imprint of St. Martin's Press.

Library of Congress Cataloging-in-Publication Data

Fo, Dario.
    My first seven years (plus a few more) / Dario Fo ; translated from Italian by Joseph Farrell.—1st U.S. ed.
        p. cm.
    ISBN-13: 978-0-312-35917-1
    ISBN-10: 0-312-35917-9
    1. Fo, Dario—Childhood and youth. 2. Authors, Italian—20th Century—Biography. I. Farrell, Joseph. II. Title.
                                        952
PQ4866.O2 Z463413 2006        Fo
852'.914—dc22                 11/06
[B]                                             2006046326

This translation first published in the United Kingdom by Methuen Publishing Ltd

First U.S. Edition: October 2006

10  9  8  7  6  5  4  3  2  1

# PROLOGUE

What I propose to tell is not the story of my life as an actor, author and director, but rather a fragment of my childhood. To be more exact, only the early part of it: the prologue to my adventure, starting from the time when it would never have entered my head that I would end up plying my trade as a performer.

I remember Bruno Bettelheim, author of a revolutionary theory on the formation of the character and intellect of the individual, saying: 'All I ask is that you give me the first seven years of the life of a man. It's all there; you can keep the rest.'

I have gone over the score a bit: I am offering you ten, plus a couple of pointers towards the years of my maturity . . . take my word for it, it's already too much!

# CHAPTER I

## The Discovery that God is also supreme head of the Italian State Railway

Everything depends on where you are born, a wise man once said. I have to say that in my case he got it absolutely right.

First of all, I have to say thank you to my mother, who chose to give birth to me in San Giano, on the shores of Lake Maggiore. Odd metamorphosis of a name: double-faced Janus, or Giano, one of the gods of ancient Rome, transformed into a completely invented Christian saint who was, into the bargain, the alleged protector of the *fabulatores-comicos*. To be truthful, the choice was made not by my mother but by the Italian State Railway, who decided to dispatch my father to perform his duties in that station. Yes, my father was station-master, even if he was not a native of the place. The San Giano stop was of such negligible importance that all too often engine drivers swept by without so much as noticing. One day a traveller, tired of having to get off at the next station, pulled the emergency cord. It took some time for the brakes to engage, and the train drew up right in the middle of a tunnel. A goods train coming behind ploughed into the back of the stationary train. Miraculously, there were no casualties, and only one serious injury – to the passenger who pulled the emergency cord. The wretched man had the misfortune to be severely beaten up by all the other occupants of the carriage, including a nun.

With the arrival of my father, everything at San Giano station changed utterly. Felice Fo was the sort of man who commanded respect and deference. When he took his stance on the railway line, erect and upright, red bonnet just above the eyeline, clutching the matching red flag, every single train, whether grand express train or local puffer, of which there were four a day, drew to halt.

I came into the world in that subsidiary stop four steps from the lake (*Ante-lacus*, in the words written on a Roman tablet), between a local train and a goods train. It was seven o'clock in the morning when I made up my mind to peep out from between my mother's legs. The woman who acted as midwife hauled me out, held me up by the feet like a chicken, then, very swiftly, gave me a great slap on the buttocks . . . and I squealed like an alarm call. At that very moment, the six-thirty passed by . . . a couple of minutes late, obviously. My mother always swore that my first howl was far louder than the whistle of the locomotive.

So, I first saw the light at San Giano solely by decision of the Italian State Railway company, but that was my place of birth only in the eyes of the Registry of Births, Marriages and Deaths.

In my own eyes, I came into the world and came to awareness some thirty or forty kilometres further north along the lake, at Pino Tronzano, and then some years later at Porto Valtravaglia, on the narrow strip of land flanking Lake Maggiore. Both of these were my 'wonderlands', the places which unleashed my wildest fantasies and determined every future choice I would make. The various moves were made courtesy of the executive of the Italian State Railway, Milan division.

Milan! I remember going there for the first time with my father. I was very young and he was there to take some exam or other in rail traffic control in the hope of being promoted to station-master, second class, category C. So why did he bring along a child of my age? I have always suspected that he took me with him as a magic charm. Everybody in the family was convinced that I brought boundless good luck. As it happens, I was born in a shirt, as the saying went, that is, I emerged wrapped up in my mother's placenta, a harbinger of good fortune according to the age-old traditions of the lakelands.

When we got to Milan, shortly before entering the great hangar of the *Stazione Centrale*, the train slowed down to walking pace. Papà Felice – Pa' Fo, as my mother called him – rolled down the window and made me lean head and shoulders out. 'Look up there,' he said, pointing to an overhead bridge on steel girders, under which all the trains had to pass. I saw a huge walkway crammed with lights trained in all directions, and a series of glass cabins lit up by bright, coloured lamps. The whole amazing structure was supported by giant pylons.

'What is it?'

'It's the operational headquarters that controls the movement of all trains, as well as the points and the signals.'

At that moment, I was convinced: that glass cabin with its shining lights must be the abode of God and all the saints of station-masters. I had no doubt: our Heavenly Father was none other than the Director General of the Italian State Railway company. It was He who oversaw the placement of railway-men and the movement of trains, He who planned the engines and the birth of station-masters' children!

But let us go back to the first move from San Giano to the station at Pino Tronzano, on the Swiss border. All the family furniture was loaded onto a goods wagon for a journey which was no more than an hour and a half. I was overwhelmed by the sight of the beds and cupboards being dismantled and, believing they were being broken apart, I burst into tears of despair. My father did all he could to reassure me: 'As soon as we get there, we'll put everything back together in no time, you'll see.'

Alas, as our things were being loaded, the cast-iron stove tumbled off the carriage and smashed to pieces, causing my mother to let out a dreadful scream. I took her hand and to comfort her said: 'Don't worry, as soon as we get there, Papà will stick it back together.' Ah, the good old trust in fathers!

The coach was attached to the train and we all clambered aboard. When we got to Pino Tronzano, our goods carriage was detached and, with the help of two porters, my father and mother started to unload the parts that had to be reassembled.

I was literally fascinated by that place: the station was bigger than the one where I had been born. We lived above the station, on the first floor, and the lake lay a hundred metres away, down a steep slope. Behind us, a rocky wall with a zigzagging road cut into the cliff and climbed up to a village of fifty or so houses piled one on top of the other, as in a Romanesque bas-relief. The village contained an ancient tower, a belfry standing over the church and a large palace which housed the town hall, the school and the medical centre.

My parents and the porters were still at work when the priest turned up to welcome us and bless each of the rooms and freshly plastered walls of the house. He came accompanied by an altar boy with hair as red as his soutane, and after the due benedictions, the altar boy led me off to an open space behind the station to inspect a big compound, in the middle of which stood a massive hen run, shaped like a pavilion and packed with cockerels and hens who greeted us with festive din. Behind the pavilion, there was a row of cages which seemed to be jumping with the endless scurrying of rabbits crammed into a kind of cloister.

My father had been called to take charge of the station in succession to an elderly colleague who had recently retired. 'It's all yours,' said the altar boy addressing my mother, who came on the scene at that moment.

'What do you mean?'

'It is yours by law, the same as the points and the whistles.'

'Listen here, ginger, you're at it, aren't you?' At this point, the altar boy, never at a loss for words, was about to go into details about the origin of this unexpected inheritance, but the signalman arrived and took over from the lad. 'The station-master who was here before you,' he recounted, 'was an absolute fanatic for animal breeding. He spent more time in the hen house than in the telegraph office. These creatures breed at an alarming rate, so when he was pensioned off and had to move out, he left all these creatures to the newcomers, that is to yourselves.'

'Oh, thank you, a real godsend,' my mother exclaimed.

'Yes, sure is a fine gift, but I'll be curious to see how you manage to deal with this lot,' continued the signalman. 'Apart from the fact that every day at least half a dozen of them will scarper, one or two are sure to end up on the line just when the trains are due.'

'Well, I hope at least part of the carcass can still be salvaged,' was my mother's comment.

'Your only problem,' came back the guffawing reply, 'is to make up your mind whether to serve rabbit stew or roast rabbit. That's all there is to it.'

You will by now have guessed that our station was completely isolated. The only inhabitants were ourselves and the district signalman, who also looked after the points, and his wife. Down below, at the foot of the embankment, facing the cliff which rose from the depths of the lake, stood the police station with mooring for a motorboat and a little light-boat called *Torpedine*.

The silence at night-time was interrupted only by the steady beat-beat of the pump which drew water from the lake to fill the huge tank that supplied trains in transit to and from Switzerland. I was unduly fond of that humming sound: it seemed the very heart of the station, calm and reassuring.

Another pleasing sound was the screech which announced the arrival of a train. Sometimes the whistle of manoeuvring trains woke me up, but I had no problem in getting back to sleep, totally contented as I was. I can say that I grew up with the rattle of railway carriages and the creaking of brakes in my head, while my mind's eye was filled with the flashes of light from the *Torpedine* sparkling on the water, on the sky and on the mountains before creeping in through the window shutters.

Since we were on the border, there was always a problem with smugglers or desperate people trying to cross secretly in the goods carriages. Every train waiting in the station had to be searched by police and customs, and my sleep was often disturbed by the signals conveyed by the whistles and flash lights of the detachment on duty. I couldn't sleep through the banging on the sides of the carriages, the slamming of doors and the orders to check more thoroughly such-and-such a coach. Then the shouted signal: 'All clear!' I would be lying tensed up throughout the inspection, and only when I heard those words could I breathe freely. I always imagined some man or boy clinging onto the underside of a coach, finally able to get away to the other side. I fell asleep with a smile and a sigh of relief.

We are in 1930. The refugees in transit were usually persecuted anti-Fascists trying to reach Switzerland or France. I remember one particular night when I awoke with a start after hearing shouts, orders and a shot. I rushed to the window and peered out at what was going on below. They had seized a man fleeing the country and were dragging him off to the police station. The next day I saw them throwing him onto a truck bound for Luino, where the prison was. Later on, my father spoke to me about political fugitives, and although I did not understand much about it, that scene has remained indelibly imprinted on my memory, like a dark stain.

To meet boys of my own age to play with, I had to clamber up to the village. It was a sheer climb of at least three hundred metres, enough to leave anyone out of breath.

It was not hard to make friends with those children. They were huddled together in the piazza outside the church, and were more than a little curious to get to know a 'foreigner' like me. They all spoke a harsh, Swiss-style dialect, with 'z' in place of an 's', but they did not drag out their vowels as did the people in the Canton of Ticino.

To try me out, they improvised a couple of rather heavy practical jokes: as I was doing a pee down the cliff side, they tossed a cloth soaked in burning naphtha over me. It was a miracle I got away without scorching my willy. For the second test, they stuffed an enraged lizard – a *ghez* in the local dialect – down my trousers. They laughed uproariously as I leapt and tossed about in a frenzy, before managing to do a cartwheel which fortunately was enough to send the creature scuttling off.

These scoundrels were nearly all the sons of smugglers with one almost surreal exception – the gang leader was son of the local police chief. There were also two girls in the village whose fathers were customs men, but their parents did not want to see them in our company. The 'shoulder-boys', the name given to the smugglers who carried baskets with merchandise across the border on their shoulders, had other professions apart from contraband. Almost all tended flocks of goats or sheep, were woodcutters or builders of the dry-stone dykes used to shore up the fields and woods which would otherwise have tumbled into the valley at every downpour. The customs officers were very tolerant: they were well aware that the labours of the shoulder-boys were scarcely likely to bring them wealth, but every so often they would receive orders to round up one or two of them to show that they were alert, on top of the job and deserved the miserable pay they received. So every now and then, a couple of smugglers would be marched off. To me it all seemed like a game. I watched the arrested shoulder-boys going down to the railway station: they had not even a chain on their wrists and chatted away to the customs officers or police-men as though they were off to have a drink together.

I loved wandering around the high crests, or climbing up the streams which had dug out deep gullies in the rocks, cutting into the mountainside and leaving scars of ugly, crooked furrows as they tumbled down into the valley. Certainly I never went on my own. I would claw my way up behind the Pino boys who were two or three years older than me. The police-man's son was nine years old, and so had been elected leader and guide. To listen to him, you would think he knew every water channel and cave in that labyrinth . . . in fact he regularly got us lost!

Once, we were hauled out by a smuggler who heard our desperate yells. He appeared to us, in the cross light filtered through the dark overhang of the ditch, like the vision of a saint. He was the uncle of one of my friends, and by an incredible coincidence was called Salvatore (Saviour). I, as I have already said, was the smallest of the gang, and so he hoisted me onto his shoulders, and from that perch I looked down with a certain haughtiness at my companions. I believed I was the living reproduction of a fresco on the facade of the little church at Tronzano, where a giant saint carried the infant Jesus across a river. The baby Jesus is giving a blessing. Now that I had the chance, I too administered a swift blessing . . . giggling as I did so. Already a blasphemer at that age!

As we approached the village, night was falling. My worried mother had gone up to the piazza in Pino and there had met up with other mothers who were also waiting for their respective children, but none of them showed any signs of anxiety, quite the reverse, since they were accustomed to our late-coming. As we reached the piazza, they came over to their sons without a word. No comment, no reproaches. My mother lifted me down from Salvatore's shoulders, gave me a hug and asked: 'Were you afraid?' Lying through my teeth, I answered, 'No, Mamma, I had a great time.' Hugging me ever more tightly, she said simply, 'Oh, what a poor liar you are, my poor little crackpot.' ('Crackpot' was the tender nickname by which my mother regularly addressed me.)

The police sergeant stood among the mothers and, like the others, addressed no word of reproach to his son . . . but he did push him in front of him. Then, as I went down the twisty road leading to the station in my mother's arms, I made out, at the point where the road doubles back on itself, the sergeant and his son, still one behind the other, with the father aiming kicks at the backside of his son, who was hopping about like a frisky goat.

After that adventure, Mamma was none too keen on my playing about in the hills with that gang of young hooligans, but it was not her way to straightforwardly forbid me anything, so, sharp-witted as ever, she came up with a fail-safe ruse of her own. When she figured that within a few hours the inevitable 'call of the wild' would make me restless, she would lay out on the table a bundle of sheets of paper, a selection of crayons and coloured pencils and invite me to indulge myself: 'There you are, my little crackpot,' she would say, 'draw me a medley of pretty pictures.'

And I was off scrawling colours on the white page, pursuing with curling lines images which gushed out one after the other as though they had been imprinted on my memory. The more I entered into the delights of making patterns and filling spaces with colours, the more I was overcome by the sheer enchantment of it all.

It would invariably happen that after a bit my young hillside companions would turn up at the station porch and shout for me from under my window. 'Dario,' my mother would alert me, 'these little beasts of friends of yours are here. Want to go with them?'

She would need to repeat it over again. I was so absorbed in the paper before me that even the shrillest train whistle would pass me by.

'Sure you don't want to go, my darling crackpot?' she cheerfully repeated. 'Do you want me to tell them that you're not too well, or that you've got a bit of a temperature?'

'No, no,' I replied instantly. 'If you tell them I'm sick, they'll make a fool of me for a week: "Ooooh, poor little diddums." Could you not say they've taken me to Switzerland for cousin Tullia's wedding?'

'Her wedding! What are you talking about? Tullia's only twelve.'

'All right,' I said, trying to make amends, 'could the bride not be her sister Noemi . . . she's grown up.'

'Yes, but she's about to become a nun.'

'Well, then, say she's given up the veil to marry a captain in the Swiss Guards.'

'The Pope's Guards?'

'That's right. A nun can't just throw herself at the first man who comes along!'

Switzerland often cropped up in our conversation, in part because my father's sister and her husband and daughters, Tullia and Noemi, lived on the far side of the lake, in the rich lands of the Canton of Ticino. There was another cousin as well, the older son, who represented all that I wanted to be when I grew up. Bruno was his name and he was a champion footballer, a goalkeeper with Lugano, organist in Lucerne Cathedral and had been recently selected as representative of the Helvetic Republic to the Italian Government in Rome. And if that was not enough, he was also engaged to a beautiful young woman whom he brought every now and again to visit us. Among all his uncles, Pa' Fo was his favourite. They were more or less the same age. They spoke between themselves about politics, but they did so in a hushed voice: if they ever got so heated they could no longer keep their voices down, Mamma sent them outside. 'Go for a walk along the lake because as they say in Sartirana (and here she would revert to her own dialect): Light talk glides soundlessly over the water, but heavy talk sinks.'

As soon as Bruno and my father were off the scene, I would do all I could to attract the attention of Bedelià, Bruno's fiancée. Her long neck, her soft hands, her Madonna-like fingers and above all her perfectly rounded breasts drove me crazy! When she lifted me onto her lap, I felt my cheeks flush and my whole being grow faint. Yes, I may as well admit it: ever since I came into this world, I have always liked women and they have always made my head spin. On those occasions when I have been with a radiant woman like Bedelià, with that scent of flowers and fruit emanating from her skin . . . Oh God, what raptures! In her arms, I gorged on her scents with the unrestrained greed of an addict.

My mother too was every bit as fresh and beautiful as Bedelià, and maybe even more so. After all, she was only nineteen when she had me, but a mother is beyond all comparison. My mother's scents made me drool, brought on some desire to suck at her breast and a yearning to cling close against and inside every curve and crease of her body. In her arms there was neither wind nor heat. Her warmth melted every fear: I was indeed in the belly of the universe.

But to come back to Bedelià, every time that she and Bruno left, I was downcast and silent for a whole day. They set off by boat, and we would accompany them down to the pier. Their journey was short, only to the other side of the lake, where

Brissago faced us. I would stand on the passageway leading to the mooring point, following the boat as it grew hazy, leaving behind a foamy wake which dispersed as the craft became smaller and sank into the distance. But it never disappeared. In fact I could see it moor on the far shore of the lake.

Once the police sergeant lent me his binoculars. When I put my eye to it, I saw the boat and the Swiss wharf come towards me. I got Bedelià too in my sights. Then I turned my eye to the roofs and houses. 'Lucky things,' I exclaimed, 'they live in the midst of all that chocolate and marzipan.' You see, ever since I had arrived in Pino Tronzano they had convinced me that over there, in Switzerland, everything was made of chocolate or almond paste and that even the roads were coated in nougat! The one who first fed me this lie was the telegrapher in the station, who offered me a square of chocolate with the words, 'Life's not fair! Here are we nibbling miserable, tiny squares of chocolate and there they are over there, bloody Swiss, with chocolate to throw away, even onto the roofs of their houses!'

'Onto the roofs?' I said.

'That's right. Can't you see the dark red roofs they've got? That's because the tiles are made with crushed chocolate.'

'Chocolate tiles! Lucky things.' And I swallowed enough saliva to flood my system.

That bastard of a louse of a telegrapher passed the word to the signalman, customs officers, the policemen . . . each and every one of them was in on the joke about a chocolate-coated Switzerland.

'That's why,' those swine told me, 'the other side is called the fat shore. If you're good, I'm sure one day Pa' Fo will take you there. Have you got your passport? You haven't! Ah well then, you'll not be going.'

Since I had fallen head-first for this tale about the land of milk and honey on the other side, even my mother, not wanting to disappoint me, joined in. 'Bruno's coming to see us next week, and he's sure to bring you a lot of plain chocolate.'

My father had already got in touch with my cousin's father, so when Bruno arrived in his usual boat, I was standing waiting for him on the pier, near to fainting. He and his girlfriend got off, carrying a large packet. At the customs booth, the officer made them open it. I was peering in from the gangway but I couldn't see what was in the parcel. The customs officer, raising his voice, let them pass with the comment: 'It isn't really legal, but just this once we'll turn a blind eye . . .'

The couple were finally on dry land. I was so excited and curious to find out what the parcel contained that I almost failed to greet the splendid Bedelià. In our house, up at the station, the surprise was revealed. When the paper and packing were removed, there appeared a large, slightly curved tile, entirely of chocolate!

'I pulled it off my roof,' said Bruno slyly, 'and it's for you, little crackpot. Don't eat it all at once.'

I was so astonished that I could hardly breathe. 'Can I give it a lick to taste it?' I said uncertainly, and every last one of them chorused: 'Of course. Lick away!'

'God bless Switzerland,' shouted Mamma.


A full year passed before I was able to cross the lake to Brissago. I was just five, and was as excited as a grasshopper in spring. When the parish priest in Pino spoke to us in religious education classes about Adam and Eve and the Earthly Paradise, my thoughts went to Switzerland, or more precisely to the Canton of Ticino: there in the Swiss Eden lay the abode of the elect, while our side was the home of the sinners, doomed to eternal punishment!

My mother was very cautious in feeding me information about our next journey to the Promised Land. 'Maybe . . . in a few days . . .' was as far as she would go, 'if they manage to get the boat back in service, then we'll take a trip to see uncle and aunt . . . perhaps.'

That night I dreamed they had once again suspended the ferry service: my father was standing on the gangway in a state of uncontrollable rage, as happened to him on his bad days. He pulled around him an embroidered blanket (the one from the big bed in our house), raised his arms to heaven as though he were Moses, and declaimed at the top of his voice: 'Cursed lake, open up and let us pass, for the Promised Land awaits us.'

And wham! A high wind arose, the waters started to bubble as though in a great cauldron and . . . a miracle! . . . sucked upwards by the wind, the water spiralled towards the heavens and divided in two, causing the Red Sea – sorry, Lake Maggiore – to open, whereupon the entire family, followed by the people of Pino Tronzano, Zenna and Maccagno, made their way across, chanting and singing, while the customs officers shouted after them despairingly: 'Halt! Come back or we open fire! It is forbidden to cross without passport and visa.' No one paid the slightest heed. Even the peasants and shepherds from the uplands with their cows, sheep and goats made their way across.

'No, no goats! That's not allowed,' the police yelled.

The goats in reply fired off little pellets of shit as round as bronze billiard balls, and went on their way, wagging their tails behind them. What can I say? I was already dreaming in cinematic terms.

A cry of 'Wake up, wake up!' from my mother stopped me from completing that biblical dream. 'We're late, get up. The boat's here in a quarter of an hour.' I was in such a state that I put my trousers on back to front, put both socks on the one foot, spilled the coffee cup on top of the cat and even forgot to stick the paint brushes and paper into my bag. 'Hurry up, hurry up.'

The siren from the boat tying up at the mooring was answered by the whistle of a train emerging from the tunnel. The station water-pump groaned. We were at the quay.

'Careful on the gangway. You're OK?'

'All aboard.'

'Cast off.'

I went to take my place at the prow. Mamma came up to me and whispered: 'My little darling, I've got a bit of bad news for you.'

'What sort of news?' I asked, without taking my eyes off the Swiss coast as it rushed towards us.

'The roofs in Brissago are not chocolate any more.'

'Whaaaaat?' I screamed in disbelief.

'Yes, darling. The Swiss government made them change the whole lot. The order had to be carried out at once because all the children had been chewing the tiles so furiously that they were making the roofs leak . . . holes all over the place. So every time there was a downpour, the houses flooded and the inhabitants got colds or pneumonia, not to mention the fact that greedy children ended up in bed day after day with shooting pains in their stomachs.'

'How could that be? Chocolate doesn't give you a sore stomach.'

'It all depends. If the tiles are old and as rotten as those ones . . .'

'Rotten chocolate! But the tile that Bruno brought me wasn't old.'

'But that was from a new house.'

'Oh well, then, at least his roof is safe.'

'I'm afraid not. A couple of nights ago, some thieves stole the lot.'

I burst into tears of despair. 'Damn them!' I called down curses in silence. 'God damn all thieves of fresh chocolate roofs and bring down on them a landslide of old cocoa, rotten marzipan and boiling vanilla!'

I could not be consoled.


At the quay in Brissago, Aunt Maria, whom I had never seen, Uncle Iginio Repetti and my two cousins were waiting for us. I was in such a state that I did not even deign to greet them with a glance, not even a cursory *ciao.* 'What's wrong with him?' asked Aunt Maria, genuinely concerned. Mamma made her a sign to desist. 'A tragedy. I'll explain later,' she whispered under her breath.

On the way to their house, we passed a cake shop whose windows were groaning with piles of chocolate bars. Noemi, the elder of the two cousins, had gone ahead and was coming out of the shop with an enormous lump of chocolate. When she offered me some, I accepted the offer but with a severe, disdainful look which said: 'If you think for one moment that you can fob me off with a square of dry cocoa, you've got it wrong.'

My uncle and aunt's house was on the lakeside. It even had a private harbour with a long, narrow boat, a yawl. Mamma and I were given a large room with a balcony. My God, what lodgings!

I immediately asked if it was possible to go out on the boat. In Pino I had been allowed every so often onto the customs men's motor boat, but that yawl was of a different class. To say its balance was precarious is putting it mildly. You couldn't move an inch in the boat without it immediately rocking about crazily.

They lowered me on board first: the two sisters jumped in right after me, the yawl overturned and all three of us ended up in the water. 'Damn it all! I'm only five and I can't even swim.' To make matters worse, the yawl fell on top of me and I found myself trapped inside the hull, as though under a lid. I knocked, shouted, drank in gulps of water, and somehow, I'll never know how, managed to grab hold of the bar of the seat. I heard Noemi screaming; 'My God, the boy! Where has he ended up?'

Her sister replied: 'He's not in the water. I'll bet he's stuck under the boat, inside the hull.'

My uncle dived in. Together they managed to get the boat upright, and I came back to the surface, still clinging onto the crosspiece. I was spluttering like a flooded engine.

My God, life is hard in bloody Switzerland!

That night I had nightmares which made me toss and turn about in bed I don't know how often. Just as well I was in the arms of my mother, who every time I moved gave me a kiss and dried the perspiration which had soaked me through and through. 'All right, it's nothing,' she reassured me. 'Never mind these bad dreams. You're not in the water any more, little darling, there are no more lakes or boats. Go back to sleep.'

It didn't work. As soon as I got back to sleep, water came at me from all sides. The rain was lashing down, the rivers were overflowing and bursting their banks, the water in the lake was high and rising until it seemed ready to flood onto the shoreline and submerge the station, dragging the trains beneath the waves. My mother was fleeing, holding me in her arms, climbing up the steep path which leads to Pino and on to Tronzano. Pa' Fo was somewhere behind us, balancing on his head the huge copper tub we used as a bath . . . It might come in handy as a life boat. This recurring dream, or nightmare, was derived from an experience I had lived through the previous year, when a real cataclysm had made the water rise to the highest levels ever recorded. It seemed that the water, rising inexorably, was determined to swallow us all up.

When I awoke the following day in Switzerland, I was almost surprised to find that my bed was not floating on the waves. A bit dazed, I went down to the kitchen for a cup of coffee only to find on the table a huge paint box, a clutch of brushes and a sketch pad to paint on. They were not children's toys but professional material, real painter's equipment.

'Are these for me?' I asked hopefully.

'Yes,' replied my uncle, with a laugh.

I hardly recognised him. He was dressed as a soldier: green uniform with red edgings, boots and hat complete with visor. 'Uncle, are you off to war?'

'No, it's my ordinary uniform. Didn't you know? I am a sergeant in the town gendarmes.'

It was only then that I noticed the pistol in the holster of his belt. 'Are those yours too?' I asked, pointing to a trombone and a rifle with a bullet-holder displayed on the wall.

'They are. I play in the police band, and this is my official rifle. Don't ever touch it.'

He then picked up the paint box and emptied all the paint tubes onto the table. 'See how lovely they are. They are from the Le Frank firm, a famous brand. When I was your age, I always dreamed of having paints like these. Did you know that I still paint sometimes? Have you every tried painting with colours and brushes like these?'

As he spoke, he squeezed tube after tube onto a big plate, showing me how to prepare a palette. He dipped his brush into the burnt sienna colour, handed it over to me, filled a cup of water and, setting it down on the table on a piece of cardboard, issued the peremptory order: 'Right, then. Let me see if you really are the infant prodigy they say you are.'

It is easy to imagine the outcome. In my excitement I splashed paint left, right and centre. My idea was to depict the previous day's incident with my cousins falling into the water, the boat capsizing and me ending up underneath, flailing about desperately. Instead, disaster upon disaster, nothing whatsoever of the story emerged from the hotchpotch on the page. A queue of onlookers formed, peeping over my shoulder. The whole family was there, including my mother and four gendarme colleagues of my uncle's, all arrayed in uniform with their trumpets and trombones. They vied with one another in their enthusiastic comments on my artistic skill. 'He's a real artist! I've never seen a monster like that.' 'What is it, Noah's Ark?' 'No, it's the naval battle of the Malpaga family against the Borromeos.'

At the time I was sure they were churning out these flattering words only to please me, but a dozen years later, when I was already a student at the Brera Academy, I went back to visit Uncle Trombone (as everyone called him), and happened to see that painting hanging on a wall. They had even gone to the trouble of having it framed. I realised then that it was a fine piece of work. It looked like a Kandinsky! Who knows how I would have preened myself if I had been aware of that earlier but, both fortunately and unfortunately, candour and consciousness never take up residence in the same person at the same time.

In any case, that first week in Switzerland was unforgettable. I had the luck to be there during the festival of the Free Cantons. An assembly of people in period costume gathered in the piazza: first came those in gold and blue embroidered tunics playing the part of the tyrannical dukes, behind them in the procession the German soldiers, then the noble ladies and finally the patriotic rebels led by William Tell and his son. In the centre of the square, against a wall decorated with a bas-relief motif to signify a portal, stood a small boy with an apple on his head. William clutched a cross-bow, aimed it at the boy but a woman shouted: 'No, my son, nooooo!' It was the boy's mother who obviously had little faith in the much-heralded accuracy of her husband. The point of that scream, I learned years later, was to distract the audience's attention momentarily from the boy with the apple on his head. Taking advantage of that brief loss of concentration, the portal with the boy in front of it swung on its own axis. The real child disappeared, and a dummy of the same dimensions, same costume and face as the boy appeared in his place. Only the very smartest saw the trick, and at five years I was not even an apprentice smarty. In a flash, William Tell fired the arrow, piercing the apple, yells from an ecstatic public, end of show. 'But what does it all mean?' I asked my mother, who before the performance had tried to recount to me the sequence of historical facts. 'It's an absolute outrage,' I exclaimed in indignation. 'It's always us children who end up in the middle of these things! The Baby Jesus is born in a stinking stable, with the roof falling in, no heating or stove, so he's got to make do with the breath of an ox and ass. Herod, who knows why? wants him dead, and so goes off and slaughters all the children in the country as though they were goats. God Himself, just to teach poor Isaac a lesson, orders his father to chop off his head with an axe. Are we supposed to be impressed if He changes his mind and comes out with a "Stop right there! It was all a joke, a godly joke!" And to crown it all, this apple on the poor Swiss boy's head, so that if Tell's aim is out, his head is going to be split open. It's him, the boy, who is the real hero but nobody even remembers what he's called. The feast is in honour of his father, the idiot who put on the bet in the first place.'

To tell the truth, my indignation did not last long because at that moment the mounted gendarme band came on the scene. I let out a cry of amazement. My uncle, mounted on horseback like the others, was one of the musicians, and was blowing into his trombone with big oompas which resounded all over the square. I was puffed up with pride: in my eyes, the reputation of my gendarme uncle soared at the very least up to the stars!

The following day Mamma had to return to Luino, and to cheer me up Noemi took me with her to the kindergarten where she worked as nursery nurse. I found myself surrounded by a pack of children more or less my own age but who came mainly from the Cantons of the Léman, so they were Swiss-Germans, without a word of Italian. I attempted to communicate in the Lombard dialect, but they looked at me as though I were crazy.

After a while, we were all taken into a big room dominated by an organ. A large lady, who seemed to be made of butter and cream, was seated at the keyboard and began to play. Another woman, pedalling the bellows with all her might, was seated beside her. A sound worthy of a cathedral emerged from the pipes, and the children's chorus gave voice to a magnificent hymn, the aria rising to a crescendo as it was repeated with only minuscule variations. Once I had got the hang of it, I joined in the chorus, at first quietly, then with full-throated gusto. I even imitated the words, pretending I had them at my fingertips: '*Antzen ut Schivel mit nem lauben troi wirt . . .*' God knows what sort of fantastic tale I was recounting.

A few days later, Uncle Trombone presented himself on horseback in the open space in front of the house. Noemi heaved me up on the animal's back or, more precisely, onto its neck. I was beside myself with joy. 'Come on, let's go and visit Bruno in Lugano. He's expecting us.' A hour's journey on horseback with a gendarme uncle! A super-luxury marvel!

We did not go down the usual roads, but cut along the byways, beside the fields, through the woods. At one stage we were almost attacked by a swarm of bees. My uncle put his gendarme's hat over my head and took off his jacket to cover my legs. 'Put your hands in here too. Unfortunately, with your delicate skin, the bees will eat you alive,' he said.

'Who said Switzerland was an Earthly Paradise? It's a terrifying place.'

To make matters worse, the horse was stung by those ravenous bees, got excited, neighed as though preparing for a lance-at-the-ready charge, pawed the ground twice and set off at full gallop! Uncle did his best to restrain him, but who could restrain the bees? They came after us as far as they could but after a time had to give up, allowing our champion to slow down, even if he still kept his neck arched and trotted like a great victor.

I would never have expected such warmth of greeting from my cousin who was standing waiting in the front of the church with some friends and . . . Bedelià and several other girls. Almost all splendid girls but – needless to say – none who could stand comparison with her!

'Why are we going to church?' I asked.

'It is a very special church, where they give concerts, and there are some Italian musicians there. Come and I'll introduce you. They are all exiles.'

'Exiles. What does that mean?'

'It means they all had to flee Italy to escape imprisonment.'

'Ah, just like the men who hide in the carriages at Pino. Refugees, in other words.'

'Exactly. The very same. These particular ones are all anarchists.'

Obviously I had no idea what 'anarchist' meant, and that was not the time to ask for explanations. We were late, and the concert was about to get underway. I took my seat in the best place in the world – Bedelià's lap, where the chair back and headrest were her breasts!

The musicians were warming up, and Bruno was seated at the piano. There were guitars as big as a man (called double-basses), great twisted trumpets (the saxophones), drums with plates and metal tambourines (percussion), and then trumpets more or less identical to those in the gendarme band. The musicians also included two black men with a curious guitar and a woman with a violin. Bedelià explained to me that that the violin was called 'hot' and that the round guitar was a ukulele.

'When are you coming back to see me on the other side of the lake?' I asked her.

'I'm afraid it's going to be a bit difficult. The Fascist government has made our government withdraw Bruno from the embassy because of his somewhat subversive ideas.'

I was on the point of asking her what 'subversive' meant, but the concert was beginning, so silence and attention.

I had never heard music like that before. At first, it seemed to me like an off-key racket, or like the high-pitched trumpet sounds that clowns make, but then I found myself beating my hands to keep time. A ramshackle harmony was emerging from it all, and I was enjoying it.

'What do you call this music?' I asked Bedelià.

'Jazz, and the one they're starting is the blues. They'll start singing in a minute.'

The two black men got to their feet and sang a few notes in a voice as powerful as a trumpet, then launched into a rhymed routine, waving their arms about and doing a few shuffling dance steps. The girl on the violin joined in the song, and Bruno, not to be outdone, produced from somewhere an incredibly guttural, mellow, black man's voice.

In no time, everyone in the stalls was swept along by the singing. Gradually, even those highly reserved Swiss folk were raising their arms and swinging them about in imitation of the gospel singers in the transept: they were clapping their hands, stamping their feet and singing along to the various refrains. I certainly had no idea at the time, but I was present at one of the first jazz and blues events in Europe.

They say that as children our senses are as receptive as photographic plates: every colour, every tremor of emotion is imprinted with unbelievable depth and precision. That event must have affected my way of hearing music, leaving it inscribed not merely as a sequence of notes and rhythms but as a ritual gesture and collective action.

When, a week later, I returned to Pino, my mother asked me what had happened to me. I launched into an account of what I had seen – of my song in German, the horse enraged by the bees, and when I got to the jazz concert I tried to reproduce the sounds by shaking my arms and legs like a grasshopper.

'My little darling,' my mother said in genuine concern, 'are you sure they didn't drug you? Were you bitten by a tarantula or bewitched in some way? Calm down, take a deep breath and above all don't tell a soul around here about the anarchist exiles who were playing and singing with the Negroes. It's dangerous!'

It is 1932, I am six years old and have to go to school. My brother Fulvio was two years younger than me, but it was unanimously agreed that he gave proof of extraordinary intelligence. At four years, he could read and write like a child twice his age. In addition, he was liable to come out with witticisms and observations that left people gasping.

The primary school in Pino was nothing special: there were only three classes, and to carry on with their schooling, pupils had to go to Tronzano, some six hundred metres higher up. In Pino there was only one teacher in charge of ten boys and seven girls. Her name was Sister Maria, a nun in the order of Saint Vincent, and she wore a white headdress tied under her chin. For me, she was like the Great Earth Mother: generously built, majestic, gentle and filled with tenderness towards everyone. She never raised her voice nor her hand to any of us, not even when we fully merited a slap on the cheek or a kick on the backside. I was bewitched by Sister Maria, the more so since I was her favourite, even if she concealed it. Perhaps I behaved like a real teacher's pet, always turning up with some flowers which I had picked on the hillside. Once I arrived with a little rabbit which I had dragged out of the compound, but on another occasion I went right over the score: I brought in an ugly, filthy stray dog.

On each occasion Sister Maria let out squeals of joy, and seemed as delighted as a little girl. And let us say nothing about her expressions of amazement when I showed her one of my paintings. She frequently encouraged me to draw or paint in class, and did her best to get all my classmates involved.

Our school was housed in the old, medieval town hall. Outside, in the corridors, they were freshening up the paint on the walls, and the painters had left tins of oil paint in a cupboard. One of the girls happened to bring a couple of brushes and one of these tins into the classroom and, while Sister Maria was briefly out, she started to do a painting on a wall. The rest of us were shocked. 'Messing up the walls like that. You're going to catch it when Sister Maria gets back!'

Sister came in just at that moment, took one look at all those smug faces and said: 'Not a bad idea! Why don't we paint the whole room?' We looked at her dumbfounded. 'Dear, dear, Sister Maria has gone off her head.'

The first girl, with a look of triumph, got on with splashing colour on the classroom wall. A moment later, each and every one of us, like crazed ants, attacked the walls, brandishing brushes dipped into the paint tins we had thieved.

That winter, it snowed more than usual, so to get to school we had to put on skis. My brother Fulvio and I had learned to use those contraptions fairly quickly, but these were not the kind of skis that people are familiar with nowadays. They were wooden boards, roughly cut and attached to the boots with belts and rudimentary fasteners. They were not intended for sporting purposes, but only to allow us to move about without sinking in the snow. The ski poles were staffs of ash with two little circles of wickerwork fixed onto the bottom.

It took real talent to move with skis like those, but all of us in the valley must have had an abundance of it, since we managed to hurtle down some of those breathtaking slopes without breaking our necks.

Towards February, when no one expected it, there was a tremendous snowstorm which left a covering of snow a metre deep. The lorries could no longer get through, and the railway, too, was blocked. There was a snowslide between the two Zenna tunnels and the snow made the road to Luino impassable. The only way to get about was by skis or sledge. As children, we had no idea what it meant to be completely cut off. It was not even possible to reach the Swiss side or the Luino shore from the lake. A north wind stirred up huge waves, causing the police motor boat to slip its moorings one night, crash into the cliff and sink.

For us the whole business was a godsend. The need to ski everywhere, the opportunity for endless snowball fights and the adventure of finding ourselves completely cut off made us feel as though we were marooned on a desert island. The people in the valley were not unduly worried, since the grocer had supplies enough for three or four days. The butcher had access to as many sheep and goats as he could wish, and the smugglers now had a free hand. The customs men on the border posts were not able to move with any agility on the snow-covered peaks, but the shoulder-boys with their home-made skis, even when they were weighed down with baskets packed with cigarettes and other contraband goods, could manage the circus turns needed to make it across the steep mountain slopes.

That very week the rumour began to circulate that the sergeant in charge of the *carabinieri* station had been relieved of his command and ordered to move to 'another location'. Someone had snared him in the bird-trap, as the saying was, in other words, someone had written a letter to the head office in Luino accusing the poor officer of being in cahoots with the smugglers, and of turning a blind eye to the continual cross-border movement of subversives and common criminals wanted by the authorities.

A miserable stab in the back. Most people in the town were convinced that the whole squalid business had been orchestrated by the officer in the customs force, others that the report came from the vice station-master who came from Maccagno every day to relieve my father. 'He's a fanatical Fascist, that one,' Pa' Fo always maintained. 'Yes, but he'd better look out,' my father's assistant would reply. 'People are liable to slip under a train, especially with all this snow about!'

A few days later, the council workers managed to clear the tracks, and a tractor with a snow plough got through on the provincial road. We were once again free, the more's the pity.

This meant that they could now arrange the removal of the *carabiniere* sergeant: the same story of dismantled furniture, the same stove slipping off and breaking apart. The officer's wife was extremely sad: she embraced my mother and all the women in the town when they went down to say goodbye. Even Nanni, their son, the leader of our adventures and games on the hilltops, was upset and struggled to hold back his tears. I too felt a tightness in the pit of my stomach which almost bent me double.

But I knew that of all the family, the one I would miss most was Nanni's little sister, Beatrice, who shared my bench at school . . . with those big black eyes of hers . . . the one who always stole my rubbers . . . who messed up my drawings . . . who put ink on my nose, but who held my hand on the way home to the station and who went happily sliding along beside me until we ended up rolling together on the grassy verge of the road, giving each other big hugs. Often as we rolled head over heels we would bump heavily into things but then would help each other back to our feet. I would put my arm round her waist, to help support her . . . and she would kiss me lightly.

It may be that we manufactured those accidents deliberately, or maybe they were completely fake! 'But now that Beatrice is going away, who's going to roll home with me through the fields?'

# CHAPTER 2

## *The Anarchists Depart*

Quite unexpectedly, with the first ferry after the resumption of service, we saw Bruno arrive alone, without Bedelià. What had happened? Kisses, embraces . . . I hoped at least for a box of chocolates, but nothing was produced. My first thought was: 'Something has gone wrong here!' Bruno and my father communicated in low, intense whispers.

The following day, as soon as Bruno had set off for home, my mother took me aside and said to me softly: 'My darling, Papà wants you to do him a big favour. We have to get a letter to one of those friends you met in Lugano . . . you remember that church?'

'Oh yes, the one where they played and sang the black music.'

'Good for you. You'll have to join Bruno over there, and I'll stitch a letter into your jumper. The police will definitely not bother about you.'

'All right!'

'You won't be afraid . . .'

'No, not at all.' I drew my knees together so as not to let her see that they were knocking with fear. The next day they took me down to the pier, where I was entrusted to the care of the ferry captain. During the crossing, I stayed seated with a blanket over me.

'Why don't you go upstairs with the other children?' asked the head sailor. 'Is something the matter? Not feeling well?'

'It's not that. If I'm upstairs I feel like vomiting. I get sea-sickness.'

'What a pity. Someone who lives on the lake and who cannot even go out on a boat,' said the sailor.

Bruno was there waiting for me on the wharf at Brissago. He gave me a hug and together we went to get the coach for Bellinzona. The anarchists were already preparing to move out. The Italian government had made a complaint to the Swiss authorities because they had allowed subversives to set up home there, on the border. They had to pack up, get out of the Ticino and even out of Switzerland. My cousin was enraged and I heard him curse: 'Great country, this! All neat and tidy, the cleanest cesspool in Europe. They bow and scrape to every arsehole who farts out orders at them!'

From the conversation, I learned that was not the first time the anarchists had been forced to undergo that kind of violence. Around forty years earlier, in the days of the famous anarchist Pietro Gori, a large number of refugees had been forced out of Lugano. The king and government of the day had pressurised the Swiss parliament into denying those subversives the right of asylum.

We were still recalling that first diaspora when we arrived at the Caffè Lungolago. Bruno took me into the toilet, where I took off my jumper and put on another which I had in my bag. In the corridor outside, one of the anarchists grabbed the garment which had the letter sewn into it and stuck it in his rucksack. He took me in his arms, held me tightly and told me: 'Thank your father, give him a kiss when you next see him. Tell him to be careful, not to give anything away.'

'Yes, I'll let him know.'

We went out. There were lorries drawn up to carry off the possessions of these undesirables. Before leaving, they drew themselves up in a line along the quay from where they could make out Italy on the far side of the lake.

'Now they're going to give us a song.' I thought to myself, 'they'll beat time with their hands and start swaying about in a dance like last year in the church.'

Instead, to my surprise, they intoned a low, almost tearful, tune to take their leave of the lake and of the friends who had come to say goodbye. There were people from the Ticino, but also others from further afield, from other cantons. The moment the lorries and the coach moved off, they waved their hands in the air and some even applauded. I was about to applaud as well, but Bruno grabbed my arm to stop me. 'Don't move a muscle. There are policemen here from Italy in plain clothes. It's better if they don't find out who we are.'

Many years later, after the war, I heard time and again that song of the anarchists, which goes:

> *Addio Lugano bella,*
> *Oh dolce terra pia.*
> *Cacciati senza colpa*
> *gli anarchici van via.*

> Farewell fair Lugano,
> Gentle, blessed land.
> Expelled without guilt
> The anarchists take their leave.

I have sung that song many times myself, but I have never managed to get to the end. At some point, my voice always turns hoarse, and I can only pretend to be singing. Each time, I find myself back there, on the quay, a boy once more, attempting to applaud while my cousin holds me back: 'Let's try not to stand out.'

# CHAPTER 3

## The French Friend

Years later, in the summer of '44, as the Second World War was drawing to a close, a man came from France to visit us, and he embraced my father with incredible affection . . . they had been friends since their early youth and had got to know each other in Montpellier where my father had emigrated to find work on a building site. As *maguts*, that is boy-masons, they had every day climbed together up the scaffolding of big houses under construction.

In those days, in 1913, bitter disputes were underway to secure workers' emancipation, to win rights, a decent salary and above all safety in the factories and yards. The strikes and accompanying demonstrations were invariably broken up with unthinkable ferocity. The workers were charged not only by the police but also by the army and cavalry. However, at the end of it all, the trade unions had managed to obtain some advantages.

On the very day they went back to work on the building site, the whole scaffolding collapsed and around fifteen workers, including my father, were thrown to the ground. Ten survivors, some dying, were rushed to hospital. My father was one of the more fortunate ones: he had broken his leg in several places and a blow to his back had left him semi-paralysed.

On his release from hospital, he was taken home by Andres, as his fellow *magut* was called. Andres's mother looked after him as though he were her own son. My father often said that he owed his life to that woman.

When he was well enough, he moved to Germany, still in the company of Andres. They found employment in a site in Hanover, just as the First World War was about to break out. Andres went back to France, my father to Lombardy. Two years later, Italy entered the conflict and, still not yet nineteen, my father found himself in the front line on the Carso.

From their conversation, I discovered that the letter sewn into my jumper which I had brought to the anarchists at Bellinzona was to be handed over to him in France. Andres was then in charge of the Association for the Aid of Political Refugees, whom France had 'welcomed' in such large numbers. Naturally my father had requested Andres and his organisation to give asylum to the fugitives and to help them find work and accommodation.

Both my father and Andres had been active in the Socialist Party (obviously each in his own country) before and after the war. In those days, the workers' movement had found its raison d'être in solidarity with the persecuted, no matter which party or democratic group they belonged to.

But let us go back to my boyhood in Pino.

# CHAPTER 4

## *The Novice and Fulvio in the Mud*

At the beginning of my second year in the Pino primary school, an assistant named Irene arrived to give Reverend Mother a hand. She was not yet a nun, but a lay-sister, in other words a novice, so she still had all her hair, bunched discreetly inside the headdress. She wore a kind of light blouse several sizes too big to cover her delicate, harmonious body, and moved with great agility, swinging her skirts as though there were gusts of air coming from inside.

My brother Fulvio was not yet due to be attending school, but considering the ease with which he had picked things up, the Reverend Mother had accepted him into her class. Since we were living in such a backwater, no one would ever bother.

On 21 March, the first day of spring, it was the custom to go into the fields near the woods on a 'narcissus outing', that is, to gather great bouquets of scented narcissi.

That particular day, all of us in the school went up to Arcomezzo, where the thousands of flowers growing there seemed to have painted the plains white. We had been entrusted to the care of Irene, who seemed by far the most frisky of all of us: she ran about, jumping in the air, pulling up her long skirt and waving it here and there as though she were chasing off swarms of wasps. She told us not to restrict ourselves to narcissi but to gather cornflowers, lily of the valley and hyacinths as well. After a couple of hours, we started back down with bunches of flowers bigger than ourselves. The young novice continued to urge us on, throwing tufts of musk and clumps of wild onions at us, then skipping off with all of us in her train like so many bloodhound puppies.

The peasants had constructed low walls to prevent slippages of land, and the sister took great pleasure in leaping over them with one bound. For us it was a bit harder: cut knees, trips, tumbles.

All of a sudden, the cry went up: 'Fulvio has fallen into a swamp!' My brother had attempted to leap over a dyke and, not realising that on the other side of that pile of rocks there was a deep ditch filled with slimy mud, had plunged straight in. The young novice rushed over, white in the face. Fulvio was literally sinking in the marsh and was likely to suffocate. Irene did not hesitate one moment but jumped into the quagmire as she was, fully dressed. Even though she was in the mire up to her neck, she managed to lift my brother out and heave him onto the grassy verge.

Now she attempted to get a grip on the edge of the ditch, but each time she tried, the verges came away in her hand. There were branches lying on the ground a few metres away. We pulled the longest branch over to the ditch so that Irene could catch hold of it. All together, clutching the branch like the seven dwarves (even if there were actually twelve of us), we pulled and tugged like madmen until our novice began to re-emerge. She was caked in mud from her feet to her cheeks, and her dress clung to her body like a plastercast.

Even today I blush at my behaviour: there was my brother stretched out on the ground, half asphyxiated, bleeding from head to toe . . . and I had eyes only for that prodigious blend of garment, mud and girl's body on which all the various round and smooth forms could be made out more clearly than if she had been naked.

After a few moments, I realised that I was not alone in appreciating that prodigious metamorphosis. One of the girls cried out: 'Irene, you're gorgeous! Your breasts and the little whatsits are sticking out.'

The novice did not seem unduly worried. After all, we were only children, so no scandal. Her only concern was with the injury to Fulvio's neck, which was cut deeply and was bleeding. She picked him up in her arms and ran with him towards a nearby farmhouse where there was a trough in the yard with water from a stream. She jumped right in with the boy in her arms and began washing him from the neck down, swaying with him from side to side, trying with this little game to get him over the shock which had left him speechless.

Shortly afterwards, the farmer's wife came down from the house above the stables, from where she had seen everything. She had understood the nature of the problem and so came armed with sheets and blankets. She was accompanied by a little girl whom, when she saw the blood pouring from Fulvio's wound, she sent to the kitchen to fetch linen bandages and some alcohol. Irene then handed Fulvio over to the care of the woman and, water dripping everywhere, clambered out of the trough: with the sheets and blankets pulled around her, she ran over to the stables.

My poor brother meantime was screaming like a bald buzzard as the woman disinfected his wound. A few moments later, wrapped up in the blanket, the novice emerged from the stables. My brother, with his head swathed in bandages, was parcelled up in a canvas sheet.

That seemed to be the end of the adventure, but three days later Fulvio took a turn for the worse. He turned pale, his face the colour of a rag, and was vomiting and running a temperature. The doctor came to Pino three days a week, and had left just that morning. The doctor in Tronzano had had to rush to Luino where his mother had suffered a heart attack. My father wired a cable to the station at Maccagno six kilometres away: 'Find me a doctor.'

'There is one, but he's out doing his rounds and we can't trace him,' came back the reply.

All the while, Fulvio was deteriorating. His temperature had reached forty degrees, and there was no way of knowing what had happened to him – congestion, intestinal infection or meningitis? It did not occur to anyone to think of the injury to his head.

Mamma continued placing cold patches on her son's head and warm ones on his feet, but finally gave up and threw herself on a chair in despair. 'My son is dying, and no one is coming to help us,' she moaned between her tears. 'We've got to get a car to take him to the hospital in Luino.'

'Here's the butcher coming in his van,' said my father, trying to reassure her.

She paid no heed, but sat uneasily in a trance-like state, as though listening to someone talking to her, then gave a serene smile. She turned to my father: 'You can calm down now, it's going to be all right. Someone will be here in a moment to save him.'

'Who's coming?'

'A very good doctor, on his motor-bicycle.'

'Motor-bicycle!'

'Yes, my grandmother has just told me. She was here a moment ago.'

My father patted her cheek. It was clear that despair was causing his wife to lose her mind.

'Here he is now!' Mamma leapt to her feet and rushed to the window. 'It's him!'

A motorbike had drawn up in the square in front of the station, and a police sergeant and a gentleman carrying a small case dismounted. They hurried up the stairs, the sergeant arriving first. 'A stroke of luck! Here's the doctor from Mugadino. I'd gone into the chemist's to ask if they knew where the general practitioner lived, and I met the man himself just as he was leaving.'

'As a matter of fact, we were expecting him,' said my mother with total naturalness, 'but from my grandmother's description I had no idea you were so young. Please come in. It's my son. His temperature has gone up to forty degrees.'

The doctor examined him, sounded his chest, tapped him all over his body. When he touched him on the skull, Fulvio gave a groan and shook his head. The doctor took a pair of scissors from his bag and began snipping the boy's hair. In no time I saw my brother with a tonsure, like a monk! The doctor disinfected the bald patch with red liquid, picked up his scalpel and cut into the wound. Fulvio gave a scream like a train coming out of a tunnel. A few moments later, the doctor took his temperature, which fortunately had dropped considerably. He was out of danger.

'It was a very serious infection,' was the doctor's comment. 'There was the risk of pernicious septicaemia, and maybe even worse. I'll be back tomorrow to change the medication. I have left some gauze in the wound to clean it out. Give my good wishes to your grandmother. I'm really sorry but I don't seem to remember where I met her.'

'Nowhere,' replied Mamma.

'What do you mean?'

'She died three months ago, and she's never been here.'

The doctor fell silent . . . at that moment, he believed he had a mad woman on his hands. My mother went on with her explanation: 'You see, I was on this seat, and my grandmother was sitting over there, on the bed, near my son. She spoke to me with a smile on her lips. "Pinin, Pinin, it's me . . . don't worry. Stop crying. A doctor will be along shortly, an excellent doctor, a professor of surgery . . . he's travelling by motorbike, and in next to no time he'll have your son as right as rain." '

My father tried to wave the whole business aside. 'Poor thing, she's been hallucinating.'

'It is odd,' said the doctor. 'Surgery is indeed my specialism. I am not the general practitioner, I was in Mugadino to visit my own father . . . it's him who is the local doctor there. I am doing my specialism in Milan, at the Fatebenefratelli hospital, and I do hope to go into teaching. It is curious that your wife, even granted that she was in a state of trance, could have got all these details right. Very curious, worth researching, I would say.'

'Not as a fairground attraction, I hope,' laughed my mother. 'To tell the truth it's not the first time this has happened to me. Before my grandmother died, I received news from a sister who died in childhood, and at other times from a great-grandfather whom I have never known.'

'Let the doctor get on his way. We've already put him out enough, getting him to rush round here.'

'My husband's right. You must think I'm paranoiac, the way I'm buttonholing you, but I'm not mad.'

'That's what all mad people say,' Papà cut in.

# CHAPTER 5

## My Grandparents

I had two grandfathers. The first, my father's father, was a giant of a man, almost one metre ninety in height. By trade he had always been a stone mason, like his father, grandfather and great-grandfather before him. In his village, he was known as *Maister*, in the sense of 'master builder'. My father, too, as I have already mentioned, started life as a mason, and only after the 1915–18 war did he enrol at a technical institute and take up work on the railways. 'We can drift into the most outlandish professions in this world,' my father often remarked with ill-concealed pride, 'but come what may we will remain a race of stone masons.' His word for stone mason was *comasin*, which does not mean masons from Como but comes from *faber cum macina*, that is, workers who operate using machines – scaffolding, mobile frames, cranes, winches and so on. Perhaps mechanical thinking has insinuated itself, alongside a story-teller's taste for paradox, into my DNA, so that I constantly find myself torn between rational rigour and the most weird surrealism.

When I was a boy, this predisposition manifested itself in the enjoyment I felt in taking hold of a stone and trying to modify its shape with chisel and club. I got the same sensation from kneading clay.

The many moves that my father was forced to make brought us to Oleggio, near Novara. Nearby there was a kiln alongside a brick and tile factory, and that's where Fulvio and I spent a large part of the day. We won the confidence of the manager, who not only taught us the techniques of mixing and baking but also let us work on the potter's wheel used for shaping vases. It was a truly magical game: the wheel was not only for vases, flasks and bowls, but if you had the technique to manipulate it correctly, you could adapt it to produce more complex forms, like a head or even a torso with chest, stomach and buttocks.

However, to my enormous distress, we had to move on from Oleggio as well. In fact I had to go by myself since my mother was expecting another child (who turned out to be a girl), and could not cope with both Fulvio and me. So, to give my mother peace during her pregnancy, I was dispatched to my other grandfather in Lomellina, in Sartirana.

The nickname of the Sartirana grandfather was Bristìn, which means 'pepper seed'. It did not take me long to find out the reason for that 'title': my grandfather's comments and jibes stung the tongue and stomach of anyone who had to swallow them.

I was really annoyed at having to stay who knows how long in that flat land without so much as a hill in sight . . . swarms of insects that bit you, clouds of midges that got up your nose and a huge marshland that they called rice fields.

But when I got to Grandfather's farm, my mood changed instantly. The first thing that met my eyes was a spacious portico skirting the wall of the house, where bunches of fruits and vegetables by the thousand hung from the arches. The whole thing looked like majestic decorations for a major feast. A huge cart horse stood in the centre of the yard. I had never seen a horse of such dimensions, one which could have easily passed for an elephant. Next to him an agile and graceful mare was performing caracols by herself, to the annoyance of a donkey which was kicking out, although more as part of a game than in anger.

An orchard with vegetable patches and an incredible variety of fruit trees opened out on the far side of the canal which cut through the farm. Grandfather Bristìn took me by the hand and together, astride the donkey, we crossed the wooden bridge over the canal. The first thing that came into view was a plum tree but, incredibly, different coloured plums, yellow, red and blue, were hanging from each branch. My grandfather explained that it was a 'multiple transplant', and was his own work.

I had never seen the like! It could have been an enchanted scene in a fairy story. A long ladder was propped against the trunk and Grandfather encouraged me to climb up: 'Go on, climb up and try one. See how each one has a different taste from the one next to it.'

And it was true. First I bit into a dark plum, and beautifully scented, red juice squirted over my face. When I tried others on other branches, I found that the yellow plums had a delicate, sweet pulp, the red ones seemed to have been dipped in rosolio, while others again were swollen and fatter with a harsh, bitter flavour. The most succulent were the tiny yellow ones which hung in bunches and had a soft stone that you could chew. I was astounded when I came across a large branch with reddish-yellow fruit . . . incredible: an apricot transplant on a plum tree!

'You're a magician, Granddad! When I tell them all at school, nobody's going to believe me. They'll tell me I'm a fibber, although they've already stuck that title on me millions of times!'

The pathways to the different nurseries were lined with myriads of plants and flowers. High jets of violet irises or blue gladioli appeared at intervals along the way, while a luxuriant bower of roses held pride of place at the crossroads in the centre of the farm. In the background, in the distance, lay the railway track: 'Thanks, Granddad, for that railway line,' I said. 'You did it to make me feel at home, didn't you?'

'Good lad,' he exclaimed. 'Very witty. You're a Bristìn as well.'

The following day, I discovered that Granddad Bristìn was a greengrocer as well. In addition to growing vegetables and fruit, he went to sell them in the town and in all the farms and farmsteads in the district. He came to wake me up that morning when it was still dark, and took me down to the kitchen, a big room with a fireplace as grand and deep as a closet in a sacristy. Five or six young men sat around the table in the centre of the room, taking their breakfast. Each of them greeted me noisily and wanted to pick me up and throw me in the air like a puppet. These were my uncles and they all had ferocious strength. Grandmother was worried and stopped them: 'Enough of that. You'll hurt him.'

Grandmother's name was Maria but they all called her *la bella Maria*. She was fifty-five and even though she had had nine children and had worked hard all her life in the fields and spinning mills, she was still worthy of the name they had given her. She was gentle and kindly, and moved with unimaginable grace.

Grandfather Bristìn was in the farmyard, harnessing the horse to the vegetable cart with the help of Aronne, his eldest son. All of them, uncles and farmhands, went over to the wagon to help load the last baskets of fruit and newly picked bunches of flowers. Granddad picked me up and placed me astride the horse's back, then handed me the reins: 'You drive,' he ordered.

'But I don't know how to, Granddad. I've never done it.'

'Nothing to it. When you want the horse to turn right, pull this rein. When you want it to go left, pull the other one. To make it stop, tug both of them together.'

'And to get it going again?'

'Let the reins go slack and bring them down on his back. Give him one or two digs with your heels and above all, you have to shout – Go! Giddy-up!'

'I'll have a go, but where are you going to sit?'

'On the cart. I'll have a little snooze.'

I was terrified. 'But at least tell me the way.'

My uncle, trying to be helpful, said: 'So that you won't get lost, here's the map with the way marked in red. You follow this route and stop the horse where you see these yellow signs. You can't go wrong.'

They were all mad in that house. For God's sake, I wasn't even seven, and they were packing me off down roads I had never seen before, with a horse and cart I had never ridden, and at the same time my grandfather was planning to snooze in the back. And now I had to read a map!

'Excuse me, Uncle Aronne, but what does this sign mean?'

'It's a bridge, a big bridge over the river Po.'

I was near to tears, but all together the whole family began chanting:

> *Il fantolino è un gran fantino,*
> *E' un carrettiere che non può sbagliare.*
> *Il nonno dorme come un ghiro*
> *e lui, tranquillo, lo porta in giro.*

What a horseman is this young boy,
He'll drive the wagon like a toy.
His granddad's sleeping like a dormouse
As they trot from house to house.

A slap on its hindquarters and off goes the horse, slowly but surely, its hooves clinking against the hard cobbles. First right . . . straight on, over the bridge . . . down to the first farmstead. Unbelievable! I've made it! The collection of houses was as big as a small town: an open space in the centre and on all four sides an enormous porticoed structure housing ten or more families. Women and children emerge from every corner and come charging over to Bristìn's cart as though they had been waiting for him. He greets them all by name and, in a tone of good-humoured ribaldry, has a complimentary or ironic joke for each one. He teases each in turn about their husbands or lovers, devises clownish bits of nonsense on their relationships, all the while throwing vegetables up in the air and catching them as they fall, like a real juggler. At the time, I did not grasp the storm of sexual, often downright obscene, allusions which my grandfather was firing off as he fiddled about with courgettes, enormous carrots and cucumbers festooned with odd bumps. His comic routine produced shrieks of high-pitched laughter, not to say hysterics in some quarters.

'Oh stop it, Bristìn, that's enough,' begged a large lady, holding her tummy. 'I'm going to wet myself.' And with those words, she hoisted up her skirt, swept it back and revealed a long stream of pee on the cobbles.

The women chose the merchandise, nearly all pre-season fruit which Grandfather obtained by cultivating them in his greenhouse. He weighed all the fruit and vegetables on his scales, always adding something extra – a few carrots, a sprig of rosemary, a big marrow or some flowers, accompanied usually by jaunty declarations of love delivered in mock poetic tones. It was clear that all those customers flocked in such numbers to his cart more than anything else to savour the show given by that merry chatterbox. I have often wondered if they ended up buying things they did not need simply to repay the enjoyment Bristìn offered them.

The ritual of sales and farce was repeated for the whole of the merchandising round. Every so often, Grandfather would make me get down from the horse's back and lift me up onto the cart, on top of the baskets of melons and watermelons. When the women asked who the child was, he would go into a rigmarole of being astounded at seeing me there for the first time. 'I have no idea who this little ruffian is, or where he came from,' he said. 'A while back, a girl handed him over to me, telling me he was my own flesh and blood. The father is supposed to be one of my five sons, but the girl couldn't remember which one. "What do you mean? How did it happen? When did all this take place?" I asked her. And the girl replied: "In the woods near the Po . . . I was walking along the banks of the river, picking mushrooms, long thin ones and little stubby ones. All of a sudden, what a bit of luck! I saw an erect one, as firm as a rod, protruding from the ground. A big juicy *porcino*! I love that kind and couldn't wait to grab hold of it, but I banged my head on the branch of a poplar tree so hard that my knees buckled and I sank to the ground. As I did so, I got skewered by this hard rod of a mushroom. A warm flame shot through my whole body from feet to brain. Ye gods, what a feeling! I stayed where I was, stunned. Then I heard a loud groan, and before my very eyes, in the thick grass, I saw emerge first a face, then shoulders and the rest of a body. Behind my bottom, I espied two thighs and two legs: 'Holy God,' I think to myself, 'a mushroom born of a man!' The youth with the mushroom, or the skewer-woman equipment, sighed and groaned: 'Thank you, pretty maiden!' And I said to him: 'What are you doing here buried in the shrubbery?' 'I was splashing about naked in the water, and had covered myself with leaves to get dry . . . I fell fast asleep, and when you suddenly plopped yourself down on my pecker, I thought I was going to die.' 'And what if you've made me pregnant?' 'We could always call him Mushroom!' " The girl said she'd had a hard time getting away from that scoundrel. "I pulled my sickle from my bag and shouted to him: 'All right. I'll give you a son, but in return I want the mushroom,' and with one chop, off it came." And here it is,' yelled Bristìn. 'Now then ladies, this is your chance!' and so saying he held up a firm, erect, ruby-red mushroom. 'This is a satisfaction-guaranteed mushroom, but don't expect me to sell it. However, I will agree to hire it out a week at a time. Plant it in your woods and fall on top of it whenever your fancy takes you.'

I need hardly say the women laughed long and hard. They joined in the fun, and went off with the mushroom, pretending to fight over it.

Lucian of Samosata said: 'Everything depends on the masters you have had. But watch out. Often you do not choose your masters, they choose you.' My grandfather Bristìn had chosen me as his pupil in clowning when he put me on the back of that gigantic nag as though I were one of the seven dwarves.

But Bristìn was no mere buffoon. One day I discovered that his orchard was an academy of agrarian science. In addition to the transplants, he had accomplished incredible marriages between different species of tomato, peperone and cucumber.

'You see,' he explained to me, while taking a sharp knife to those vegetables as though they were the bodies of animals he wanted to cut open to show me their structure, 'we've got male and female here, too, not to mention various hybrids. All of them, fruit and vegetable alike, are creatures like us. They are sensitive to fear and perhaps even pain, they feel attraction and repulsion among themselves just as men and women do. There are fruits which fall in love normally, and others which lose their head for creatures of another species. Even though I've tried my level best, I've never managed to get a persimmon and a papaya to join together in loving union!'

Professor Trangipane, who taught in the Faculty of Agrarian Science at Alessandria, was a frequent visitor, always accompanied by students who were spellbound by the practical lessons, spiced with comic turns, my grandfather imparted to them.

One day, while he was giving a lecture in the greenhouse, the sky all of a sudden turned black. Bristìn put two fingers in the corners of his mouth and let out a shrill whistle. His sons, fully aware of what was required of them, came running out of the carriage sheds. They stretched a covering, a gigantic fine-meshed net, out in a circle. Bristìn made sure everyone was involved in the operation, students and farm workers alike. Guy-ropes with pegs at the end hung down from high poles surrounding the greenhouse, and the net was laid along that line of poles. Following my grandfather's orders, the men started to tug at the guy-ropes in twos or threes. The net was swiftly hauled up and pulled out like a circus big-top to cover the glass of the greenhouse and give it full protection. Bristìn and his sons hammered in the stakes at top speed and secured the bottom end of the cover to the ground. The whole set-up was hardly in place when a terrible wind, whistling through the mesh of the net, got up, followed by thunder and lightning and a hail storm which sent chunks of ice as big as eggs bouncing off the net as though they were tennis balls. Everyone else rushed for shelter under the portico, but Bristìn took me by the hand and dragged me inside the greenhouse: 'Come and I'll show you a sight you won't forget even if you live to be a hundred.'

Under the glass, it seemed as though the world were coming to an end. As they struck against the net and bounced off it, the hailstones generated indescribable sounds, while the vibrating panes of glass produced howls which were in turns terrifying and entrancing. The flashes of lightning, reflected on the greenhouse glass, had their brightness multiplied as in a distorting mirror at a fairground.

When later at school I encountered for the first time the adventure of Dante's Ulysses, strapped to the mast of his ship, awestruck and bewitched by the special effects of sound and light organised by the Sirens, I could not help connecting that magical situation with the spectacle I had witnessed as a boy inside that crystal nursery, where the storm performed for us a concert that presaged the end of the world.

'You're a madman, fit to be tied,' screamed my grandmother with that thin voice of hers. 'Don't you realise what would have happened to you and that poor boy if the wind had blown the net away? The whole glass structure would have shattered to pieces and fallen on top of you.'

Bristìn, normally so strong and sure of himself, bowed his head before that fragile, delicate little woman. 'Yes, you're right, Maria. I was a bit thoughtless . . . in fact completely thoughtless. But to experience certain moments, you've got to take risks.'

# CHAPTER 6

## Back in Oleggio

After several months, Uncle Beniamino, the youngest of my mother's brothers, was given the job of taking me home. As I was leaving, Granddad lifted me onto the back of that great horse, Gargantua's stallion. 'We'll let him take you to the station!'

I took hold of the reins, but made no effort to manoeuvre with them. I had long since discovered that there was no point in pulling the reins up and down since the horse made up its own mind about where it was supposed to turn. For years, it had been padding at least three times a week along the same roads that led to the farms and villages where my granddad dispensed his chatter and wares. They had put one over me, but I refused to give them the satisfaction of knowing that I knew, and so I carried on unperturbed, mimicking the various actions of driving the cart.

Moreover, the horse responded to variations in routine only when its master gave orders with a shout or a jerk of the bridle. That was why on this occasion Granddad got up on the horse's back beside me: our destination was the station, which was not part of the horse's usual round.

Kisses, hugs, a lump in the throat and a few tears . . . shaking hands . . . the train moving off. I remained glued to the window the whole time we travelled through Lomellina, and I thought back to the day of my arrival in Sartirana, to the aversion I had felt towards that countryside infested by mosquitoes and midges, lined with rows of poplar trees marking the boundaries of rice fields and cut into an infinity of labyrinthine patterns by the vertical and horizontal spider's web of canals and waterways. Now those complex geometries had entered my brain like expressions of some surreal, metaphysical calm.

The guard on the train was surprised to see me riding alone in the carriage: it was not normal, especially in those days, for a child to travel on his own without a guardian, but I was used to it. Trains, railway tracks, stations were all as natural to me as breathing, drinking and going to the toilet.

On my arrival in Oleggio, all I had to do was look around and there, near the engine, red hat pulled down over his head, was my father. He came towards me, picked me up with one arm, gave me a hug, held me close to his face, whistled to the engine driver to give him the sign to move off and then announced with a big smile: 'There's a big surprise waiting for you at home! You've got a little sister . . . Bianca! You'll not believe how pretty she is, like a porcelain doll!'

She was indeed just like a porcelain doll, my little sister . . . so delicate in her features, with those big, shining eyes. They let me hold her in my arms for a little, but I had to give up almost immediately because she wriggled like a baby goat and burst into a terrible wail. Everybody gathered round her: relatives, friends, as well as the three schoolteacher sisters who lived on the landing. No one paid any heed to me or to my brother Fulvio. They seemed to be aware of our presence only when they tripped over us, so we decided to keep ourselves to ourselves. We played in the courtyard and in the wasteland among the trees in the park on the other side of the road. There they were putting up a circus tent. Incapable of minding our own business, we set out to get on good terms with the workers erecting large poles and stretching out the ropes which would support the Big Top. They soon found work for us: we were dispatched with the owner's son to stick up posters on the walls and lampposts all along the main streets.

In this way we won the right to get in free for the evening performances. We did ask our mother for permission but she was so busy with the new baby that she scarcely put up any resistance. We were first in the queue outside the Big Top, two hours before the opening. The attendant in charge of the wild animals took us over to see the cages. A good ten metres away from the animal compound, we were overcome by an odour that nearly made us throw up – the stench of the lions.

What a disappointment! An animal of such majesty, the symbol of might and courage giving off such a rancid stink. How can an emperor raise as his standard the image of that foul shitter?

'To be consistent, it really should bring its smell along with it everywhere it goes . . .' I said to the attendant. 'This is what happens to them when they are locked up . . . animals in captivity, forced to live in a cage, that's what makes them smell like that. Normally, freedom has no stench. When they are at liberty in the forests, they certainly do not pong that way. They smell the way they should, just enough to let themselves be recognised by their own kind and feared by their prey.'

That first encounter with the circus was overwhelming for both of us: lions prancing about and roaring so loudly that they made your insides churn up, elephants on parade, sometimes with movements of such lightness that they seemed filled with warm air, like giant balloons.

But the act which left us breathless every time was undoubtedly the acrobats' turn. Two girls starting off from their position up there on the trapeze, swinging backwards and forwards, leaving traces of evanescent light as they go. My God, what was that? A somersault . . . a girl upside down, with no grip, hands waving in the void . . . she's going to fall . . . no . . . a miracle! I have no idea how, but she remains hanging by her feet from the bar of the trapeze. Now, she swings across the whole arch of the Big Top, swallowed up by the spotlights' back-lighting, and then comes back into view, slender and sinuous. From nowhere, another girl appears walking on a tightrope which crosses the dome. She dances in mid-air, pirouetting and twirling.

Beneath, in the centre of the arena, a clown lets out shrill screams of fear at each turn, but now he is enchanted by the grace of the girl on the tightrope and wants to join her up there. He produces a long ladder and, without supporting it on the wire, climbs swiftly up. The rungs come away one after the other, but the clown continues relentlessly, clinging on by the sheer strength of his arms. There he is. He has reached the tightrope: with one leap he is there, on his feet, keeping his balance as he strolls along with his hands in his pockets. The girl tells him off and orders him to go away, and all of a sudden the clown realises he is suspended in mid-air and is overcome by panic. He wobbles, topples over . . . tumbles . . . grabs a hold of the girl's feet . . . an incredible sway to one side and there he is, upright once again, tenderly embracing his beautiful tightrope walker. He kisses her. Rapturous applause.

# CHAPTER 7

## *Porto Valtravaglia*

The school year had only just begun and Mamma had to take us to the head teacher to announce that since Papà had been moved yet again by the State Railway, her children would have to continue their education at Porto Valtravaglia. A week later, they unloaded our baggage, furniture and assorted odds and ends at the new station to which my father had been assigned.

An incredible town, this Porto Valtravaglia: standing on the banks of the lake and flanked by a river on either side. On the one side, a cliff as spiky and majestic as the Great Pyramid of Cheops. A lime kiln at the foot of the cliff. The port with fishermen's boats, an ancient spinning mill, two engineering workshops and, last but not least, a glassworks with no fewer than five ovens.

The inhabitants of Porto Valtravaglia were nicknamed the *mezarat*, that is, the semi-mice, in other words 'bats', a name given to them because most lived and worked by night. It was a necessity: the ovens in the glassworks had to remain operational twenty-four hours a day because, as is well known, shutting them down and opening them up again meant a break in work patterns of around one week. In addition, to get the best results from the moulding and blowing of the glass amalgam, there is no choice but to work back-to-back shifts. The same was true of the workers at the lime kiln and of the fishermen who, as is known, have to drop their nets before dawn; it was also true of the near-historic community of smugglers who, here as at Pino, operated by preference in the hours of darkness.

So it was that in the town of the *mezarat*, the hostelries, the *trattorias*, the bars and hotels never pulled down their shutters. At the Bar Garibaldi on the harbour, they removed the shutters altogether, because what was the point of them? There was a great coming and going in those places at all hours: kiln journeymen waiting for the start of their shift kept company with other night birds, including the indispensable ornament of any such locality – all types of gamblers and idlers. Finally, lined up in an orderly file at various points, there were prostitutes of differing levels, casualness and cost.

But among this host of misbegotten fantasists, the ones who commanded greatest attention and respect were beyond all doubt the story-tellers and spinners of yarns.

There was no independent profession of *fabulatore*, or story-teller, and in fact these great talkers came from every almost every walk of life in the Valtravaglia, but there was no question, and we shall shortly see why, that the greatest number came from the ranks of the glass-blowers.

These story-tellers were the pride and glory of this new home of mine. You came across them in bars, in the piazzas, on the church steps, on the benches down at the harbour. Often they spoke of events which had occurred centuries and centuries previously . . . but it was pure chicanery, that is, they borrowed mythical stories to deal with day-to-day life and with events reported in recent newspapers, adding a touch of satire and of the grotesque.

# CHAPTER 8

## *Foreigners and Strangers*

It is a curious fact that even today, more than sixty years on, anyone leafing through the pages of the Valtravaglia telephone directory will come across an unusually high number of foreign surnames. Here are some chosen at random: Gutierrez, Vankaus, Schumacher, Batieux, Besinsky. These are the grandchildren of the master glass-blowers who, towards the end of the nineteenth century, arrived at the factories of Porto Valtravaglia from all over Europe, each with his own speciality in casting, moulding and glass-blowing.

These *vetradór*, to adopt the dialect term, turned up in family groups with clearly differentiated values, trades and skill levels.

Inside each ethnic group, people obviously expressed themselves in their language of origin, but at work, in the factory, in the bars and on the street, communication was not in Italian but in an eccentric Lombard dialect, a speech which, continually enriched by new lexical additions, was transformed into an idiom without equal anywhere in the world. The valley of the *mezarat* had quite suddenly become a fantastic crucible of the most diverse, outlandish and often irreconcilable cultures, traditions, prejudices and mentalities, and yet, however much it might strain belief, there was never any manifestation of racism among those people. Certainly they made fun of each other, were even bitingly sarcastic over their respective pronunciations, stock phrases, gestures or modulation of guttural or sharp sounds, but never aggressively or malevolently so. It was genuinely funny to hear Germans, Spaniards, French or Poles railing at each other in a dialect that was already more than sufficiently abstruse and contorted.

Porto Valtravaglia gave birth to an incredible new idiom: lizard became *ritzòpora* (from the Greek spoken in the Hellespont), shepherd became *bergeròt*, the German term *tràmpen* was used in the sense of clumsy, *stappìch* of cheat, *sfulk* of muddle, *tacchinosa* of street-walker, and so on.

Obviously, as a boy I was not fully aware that in absorbing that strange melange of languages and dialects I was attending a unique university of communication, an experience which would afford me an otherwise unknown freedom to create expressive modules ad infinitum.

But let's get back to our *fabulatori*, the story-tellers of the Valtravaglia who with their language and tales made an indelible mark on my future choices and on my way of judging events and characters in both fantasy and reality.

The platforms where the performances unfolded, the idiosyncratic stages which varied with the trade of the individual *fabulatore* and the utility of the tale, were equally decisive.

The fishermen chose the porches near the harbour. We children were their most enthusiastic audience. Fidanza, the headman of a crew, would get his assistants to line us all up in a semicircle to hold and stretch out the nets which needed to be mended. Not that he forced us to do this, perish the thought! It was an invitation accepted with good grace, indeed with alacrity, and paid for by the tales they told. I was especially fascinated by the elements of paradox in those stories, and even more by the spicing of the language with bizarre terms which produced in my mind unfamiliar images which I then struggled to absorb into my vocabulary. Often I did not grasp exactly the sense of the word-play, and asked them to repeat it . . . so I ended up laughing out of turn, to the annoyance of my more attentive companions.

Beyond all doubt, my first teacher in the telling of tales was my grandfather Bristìn, but now I found myself attending a genuine masterclass for jesters, and I had the opportunity to study the most diverse techniques and forms of delivery.

At this school, I learned the structure of the original dialect, which is something different from merely speaking dialect: above all I acquired the structure of a primordial, integral language which grants you the total liberty, at any moment, to invent expressions.

The style of those *fabulatori*, story-tellers, was based on improvisation; as I have already mentioned, it was evident that their main concern was to adapt differing passages to a contingent reality. I had occasion to listen to the same story related in three or four different versions. The ability of the person recounting the story lay in his capacity to adapt it each time according to variations in events, including local incidents and laundry-room gossip. Every event, however unexpected, was immediately incorporated into the performance: an explosion caused by poachers, a shot from a hunter's rifle, the ringing of church bells . . . everything was grist to their mills.

And most of all, the story-tellers never lost sight of the moods and emotions of their listeners. If there was someone who guffawed, who reacted uncomfortably to the irony or who took it all badly, he was sure to become the target of the whole routine.

The same treatment was reserved for any spectator who seemed slow-witted or could not keep up with the comic action. Anything could be used to move things along, to bring them to life or to involve everyone in the narration. In brief, they managed to make the fantastic down-to-earth, and vice versa.

It is quite true that not all the story-tellers conceived narration as theatre, nor did I at that time link the two genres: in particular, I was not yet able to take in the vital difference between recounting and performing, and I was absolutely convinced that theatre-making had all to do with acting, the presence of several actors, scenery, sound and lighting effects . . . in short, with organised magic. Only much later, when I had already acquired considerable experience of the stage, did I realise that story-telling had been the mechanism which had encouraged me to express myself in epic-popular form. But this is a topic which merits a deeper, more detailed treatment which we will perhaps be able to dedicate to it elsewhere.

However, I was completely conscious that reality as seen by the story-tellers on the lake was reality seen through a distorting mirror, and that it was proposed by each of them using markedly differing narrative techniques and approaches.

For example, Galli – a poacher by profession – presented tragic tales with the nonchalant air of a man who analyses the details of a disaster without being fully aware that he is talking of the disaster itself. Then there was another who spoke quietly, almost flippantly, while he was fishing. His name was Dighelnò, a dialect name equivalent to 'Don't Tell Him'.

He settled down in his place at the harbour, set up his fishing rods while the children gathered round nagging him to tell us one of his absurd tales, but he remained where he was, not uttering a word, distractedly staring at the floats of his fishing lines as they bobbed up and down on the water. Then, under his breath, without warning, he would come out with three or four words which had no sense at all. 'When the wind blows in winter, the minnows get an itch in their arse.'

We would stare at him in amazement and he, still looking out over the lake, would turn his rod in the direction of the island of the Malpagas and go on: 'Look over there, you see that dark blue line in front of Cannero Castle? That's a current strong enough to sweep away even the police motor boats.'

And this was his way of introducing, without preamble, the story of an extraordinary fishing expedition of which he was sole protagonist and witness. 'Have you ever seen a line being pulled in with hundreds of bleak, chub and whitefish wriggling at the end of it?'

'No, never,' we chorused in reply.

'Ah well, I've had the honour of witnessing this spectacle. It happened right here on the quayside, one day at dawn. I was on my own, with no one for company except my rods and lines. I had been slaving away all night, getting them into good order. I had ten or so rods, four or five of them more than seven feet in length. I lashed three of the biggest ones together, hoisted them up like a mast, stuck onto the top of this mast another two rods, then another two, and so on until I had one huge shaft at least thirty metres long. The problem then was how to cast the line with a rod that size! A line at least a couple of kilometres in length, with over two hundred hooks. So what was I to do with that line? I had an idea: I laid out the line of yarn all along the street which starts at the church and goes right down until it nearly plunges into the lake. I got my brother's lorry and stuck the enormous rod right in the middle, with poles arranged around in a pyramid shape to hold it in place. As soon as I'd fixed up the equipment, I took the lorry up there to the top of the road which sweeps down . . . and away we go!, full steam ahead towards the lakeside, dragging behind me the fishing line which is now soaring up into the sky like a kite. The lorry reaches the quay: screech of breaks, and VROOOOM, the huge mast cracks like a whip and hurls the line out towards the centre of the lake, distributing the baited hooks and the floats with great precision.

'It was all just as I had expected. A wind got up from the land and pushed the bait and floats further out into the lake. The high waves made the water turn dark blue. "Here we go," I shouted, "in no time whole shoals of them'll be biting," and in fact next thing the floats were going under like ducks after fish. This is the moment. I get onto the lorry and get ready to start pulling in the line. Right! Gently does it if we're not to break the cord. I start off up the road, the pylon bends so far over that my heart skips a beat, but it holds. Pull, pull . . . fish, fish! Not a one! And yet I must have caught something! What could possibly be dragging with such force? Christ in heaven, I had caught the bells from the church tower in Cannero . . . on the other side of the lake!'

But the real master of the story-tellers was undoubtedly Ravanèl, who owed his nickname to the fact that he had a shock of bright red hair that made him resemble a *ravanello*, a radish. The stories he told were nearly all dramatisations of an event which had really occurred, perhaps even recently, and was thus still in everyone's memory. He would start off, for instance, with the tale of someone who had gone mad. They had come to take him away in the morning, dragging him down from the bell-tower where he was roosted, pissing with considerable panache on the faithful below as they walked in procession on some saint's day. They loaded him onto the specially padded van for the insane, the one which the council had made available for emergency transport to the mental asylum in Varese. The glass-blower's trade, it has been established, is a cause of silicosis, which can lead to bouts of madness. It was for that reason that the Valtravaglia could boast the highest output of madmen on the entire lake.

On this subject, I remember the story of a man who got it into his head that he could fly. There was another one about a man who used to walk around in the nude with a suit painted onto his skin. Then there was the man who had jumped off a bridge or the one who had burned down his house after hanging all his hens.

Generally madness was a pretext to talk about the people who surrounded the madman: the priest who wanted to bless or exorcise him, the doctor who said it was all a matter of sexual depression, and so on . . . right up to the mayor, the wife, her lover, the police sergeant.

The figure of the other, of the unpredictable, of the illogical has always held a fascination for me, but what interested me most was achieving mastery of the techniques of story-telling itself.

Take, for instance, another narrator who was always playing billiards, a game he loved. He was known as 'Braces': he was tall and thin, and always wore two garish, red elastic straps to hold up his trousers. He was also called 'Sorry Braces' because before every game he would put on an overall so as not to wear out his trousers by rubbing them against the edge of the billiards table. As the game progressed, using as a pretext some phrase uttered by his opponent, he would stop the game for a moment to introduce some incident, some story. He would circle round the table, eyeing the balls and telling his story at the same time, carrying on with the performance as he prepared his shot. The game no longer existed: all that mattered was the tale. He played on heedlessly, scrutinising the green table and never putting down the cue which, as he went on narrating, became his sword, lance, staff or even woman or violin: it became everything.

When talking a while back about my grandfather Bristìn, I mentioned to you his technique of throwing his products into the air and transforming them into characters. A very similar device was employed by another story-teller, a travelling salesman from the Valtravaglia called Caldera-Magnan, a Romany name. It was no coincidence that he practised the classic gypsy trade of selling or mending pots and pans, and giving them a coating of zinc. He travelled in an enormous cart, with everything scattered about inside, from brushes to ammonia, washing powder, hundreds of cauldrons, casseroles, cooking pots and zinc and copper bowls.

When it arrived, it looked like a monument invented by Alberto Savinio . . . a gigantic, two-storey construction; the spoils from the rout of some medieval army. He took up his position on the top of it, and while he offered his wares, he engaged his customers in discussion, devised stories, proverbs or maxims and produced the most extraordinary anecdotes.

But he would never say 'buy'. He never had a word to say on the issue of purchase: he displayed one pot, brought out another, drummed on them with his oaken fingers, creating a medley of sounds like a Japanese concert: ding, dong . . . bing, bong. He invented nonsense rhymes to that rhythm, going up and down the scales: 'My good friend here has a curate's arse . . . rub it up and it turns to gold.'

And as he drummed out his words, the character of the curate seemed to take shape almost as a real person: Ermanno by name, a young priest passionately in love with Fulvia, the tender-hearted mistress of the foundry owner. The poor booby had lost his head over her. He saw her go into church, slipped into the confessional in place of the parish priest and, in a situation straight out of classic farce, heard his beloved's confession. Sobbing and sighing, Fulvia reveals her love for the young priest and he, overcome by the discovery, breaks down completely, bursts into tears and so the deception is uncovered. Fulvia gasps, raises the little curtain between them and literally throws herself into the priest's arms. But it's out of the question to make love in that big box, so, trembling with emotion, they climb to the top of the belfry. He removes his soutane, she her clothes.

At this point in the story, Caldera would lay down his pot-cum-drum, pick up the bellows, move the 'heaving lung' in and out to give the impression of the passionate panting of the two lovers entwined in an embrace. Almost without missing a beat, he would go back to his pots, switch tone and turn on any wretch who dared show a lack of confidence in his wares. 'I told you, I told you you should have taken this pot: a pan I was giving away at half price . . . look at its lovely, shiny copper bottom, and there's you, a right stuffed arse, you've snubbed it, you've turned your nose up at it, so now you've got it right up your buttocks! That's what comes of scoffing. Remember what happened to those folk in Rocca di Caldé!'

At this point, he would introduce a kind of parable, naturally in dialect with a sprinkling of foreign words current in the Valtravaglia. '*A gh'era un vegio mult tiempo passao chi-loga in lu Porto, ol me cuntava me' per . . . l'es veretad, no' sluz fabule sbergen . . .*'

Halt! I see the readers' eyes glazing over. So for pity's sake, let us at once change register; and here follows the tale in a more simple, straightforward language. 'A long time ago, an old man lived here in Porto . . . every word is true, I'm no charlatan with a baggage of yarns to spin. This old man had warned the inhabitants of Rocca di Caldé, which is just above the quarry at the port, that a crack had opened in the mountain and the village was sliding down towards the foot of the cliff. "Hey, watch out," they shouted to the peasants and fishermen who lived lower down, "it's caving in . . . get out of there!"

' "Come on! Who says? Take it easy! The ground's not moving." And the people in Rocca laughed the whole thing off, made a joke of it: "Smart lot, them, eh? They want us out of here so they can get their hands on our lands and houses."

'And so they went on pruning the vines, sowing the fields, getting married, happily making love. They could feel the rock moving under the foundations of the houses . . . but they were not unduly concerned. "Normal process of settlement," they reassured each other. A great section of rock broke off and crashed into the lake. "Look out, you've got your feet in the water!" they yelled from along the coast. "What are you talking about? It's only overflow water from the fountains." And so, bit by bit, inexorably the whole town slid down until it tumbled into the lake.

'Splash, splash, plop, plop . . . houses, men, women, two horses, three donkeys . . . Unperturbed, the priest continued hearing a nun's confession . . . *"ego te absolvo . . . animus . . . sancti"* . . . plooooop . . . Amen . . . Splaaaash! The tower went under, the belfry with the church bells disappeared . . . ding, dang, dong . . . plop! Even today,' continued Caldera, 'if you peep over the tip of the rock which still sticks out above the surface of the lake, and if at that precise moment there is a thunder and lightning storm and the flashes light up the bed of the lake . . . incredible! . . . underneath you can just make out the sunken town with its houses and streets still intact and you'll see them, the inhabitants of old Caldé, still moving about as if it were a live crib . . . and they're still repeating, quite unperturbed: "Nothing's happened." The fish swim in front of their eyes and even get into their ears, but there they are still: "Nothing to be afraid of . . . it's only a new kind of fish that has learned to fly. Certainly, it's a bit more damp nowadays than it used to be," they comment, and apart from that they go on with their daily lives without a shadow of concern about the disaster that has occurred.'

When I am on stage, I gladly and readily make use of this approach and technique for developing a story, not with the same themes but with similar situations and above all with a similar atmosphere: for instance, in the fabliau inspired by the texts of *The Butterfly Mouse* rediscovered by Rossana Brusegan, or in the apologue that I based on *Lucius and the Ass* by Lucian of Samosata, the adventure of the poet who goes in search of the impossible and arrives at a town in Thessalia inhabited by magicians and wizards. Each time I recount this metaphysical, hyperclassical fable, what is the image I seek to project? I am certainly not attempting to imagine to myself, or to make people imagine, the Hellespont, Samos or Thessalia. I am firmly rooted in my native place, in its streets, alongside Lombard rivers, among the woods which are familiar to me: the mountains, skies, waters are always those of the place where I listened to my first stories. It may be that it does not all come out clearly enough, but my universe of images is there. Similarly, when I talk of the Provencal mountains in *Obscene*

*Fables*, of Javan Petro, of Icarus insulting his father Dedalus, even when I bring on stage the Chinese tiger and Tibet with its rivers and its vast caverns, or even in the despairing outburst of Medea or in the flight on the magic chariot, I never move far from the lake, the valleys and the rivers where I was born.

But I often tear myself away from the memory of these 'tales' to plunge into the texts of medieval codices and poets, a testimony of our more ancient roots, and each time I discover, not without some smug satisfaction, that there, in those writings, lie the roots of every fable I ever learned from my storytellers. Fables which are never pedantically reproduced but conveyed for our times with the ironic rhythms of a modernity which is, to put it mildly, astounding. Let one example suffice. It is the tale of a great hunting expedition, a wild, mythical hunt which took place year after year in the same valley. The hero of this great epic was presented from the outset astride his motor-bicycle, kitted out like a medieval knight. The hunter greets his friends and announces that this will be the final combat. One of the two must succumb that day: him or his prey. But who is this awesome prey? A snail!

But pause a moment. We are not talking about some run-of-the-mill, slithery mollusc. No, we are dealing with an epic, gigantic slug of the dimensions of a hippopotamus, a horrendous beast, a leftover from the Mesozoic age, which goes charging fiercely about in the three valleys between the slopes of Muceno and the forests of Musadino. The hunt was scheduled for the days when the chestnut trees were in bloom; scents to raise the spirits of any hunter and give him heart for the fight wafted abroad the length and breadth of the valley. So, off our hero set on his motorbike, rifle and spear at the ready, intent on seizing this snail which had escaped him for years both because of its extraordinary speed of movement and zigzagging abilities, and because of the slimy sludge the animal left in its wake as it fled. 'There it is! Damnation! You're dribbling your filthy mess right on the curve!' The warrior brakes, wobbles, slides and rolls, but this time he manages to induce the snail to speed up beyond its abilities, so that it takes a tumble and rolls into a ditch. It's done for. The hunter descends into the trench, sliding on his buttocks down the slope . . . he slays the still-breathing beast, chops it to pieces, loads his catch onto the motorbike, which groans under the weight of snail-flesh, and returns home. The whole town has good eating, or more precisely good gorging, for a whole week: enough portions of snail to make you sick!

Today I realise that this could have been a tale from Rabelais.

# CHAPTER 9

## *The Discovery of the Body*

I was no more than fourteen and I enjoyed a certain reputation among the many boys in Valtravaglia who put themselves forward as story-tellers. At that time, as I said a while ago, I had no idea of the ancient origin of those fables. I was repeating techniques and situations which had illustrious origins, blithely convinced they were the exclusive product of my fellow villagers.

I've already said that the travelling salesman, the fisherman, the billiards player, my grandfather Bristìn himself never dived straight into a story, but found some external pretext to let themselves be drawn into telling the tale, under the pretence that it was all happening in spite of themselves. Only many years later did I discover that getting into a subject by 'cannoning off another ball', as though by accident, was an established practice among *commedia dell'arte* actors from the time of the first Harlequin (Tristano Martinelli) right up to the classical Pulcinella of the Neapolitan songs. This was my first great lesson, the stamp of the true narrator: the opening of the tale must come about as though by chance.

I often use the same mechanism today to get shows underway, that is, I invent situations or pretexts which permit me to chat to the audience while the lights are still on in the auditorium. These can be quite elementary devices, such as: 'You're late. We were getting worried, take a seat. That lady there . . . yes, you . . . I saw you smoking furtively . . . that's right, she's crouching down under her own armpits . . . and she's puffing like mad . . . she's going to go up in flames!' I invent other pretexts, speaking out loud to the wings, to the stage-hands, electricians or sound engineers. 'Could you tone down that spot light. That echo's coming back again,' then I turn to the audience, 'Don't you think there's a kind of boom in my voice . . . a ricochet?' Everything can be used to smash down the fourth wall, anything to get over the cliché of 'let's see if you can make me laugh . . . let's just see if you're all you're cracked up to be'.

I also start off with a comment on something in the news that everybody will be familiar with. I often launch straight in: 'Seen today's papers? According to the headlines . . .' The intention is to disorientate the audience who have turned up expecting to see a play or listen to a story, maybe one taken from the ancient Greek narrators. Instead I wrong-foot them and start babbling about a recent, contemporary event: 'Just before I came on, I heard on the television that the sea water in the Adriatic is so pure that it's drinkable . . . all that gunge is not actually poisonous . . . research in Japan has shown that it's full of nutrients, so they have been feeding it to their turkeys, who are very keen on it. A German scientist has found it's a wonderful remedy for diseases of the skin . . . better than mud baths. In Riccione, they've set up a recuperation centre with baths filled with the gunge. The Germans are flocking in.'

But let us get back to Lake Maggiore. Performers could not have failed to include a place like the village of the *mezarat*, with its intense nightlife, in their schedules, and every week there was a visit from a different touring company. There was a theatre in Porto Valtravaglia, and another three in nearby towns (Caldé, Muceno and Musadino). In summer, acrobats and puppet shows also came to town.

From time to time I put on shows of my own for my school-mates. I repeated the stories told by Magnan, Braces and Dighelnò, with some variations or adaptations of my own. Almost without being aware of it, I was acquiring a command of the trade and building up a small but dedicated following. Having people to listen and come along when you perform is the first and essential condition. If the person performing does not savour the effervescence which spectators bring, or that involvement with other people produced by shared laughter, there is no point in him even thinking of becoming an actor. Spectators suggest to you rhythms, timing and harmonies; they make clear to you the lines to cut, or that it is useless per-severing with a particular situation.

The audience has always, at every stage, been my litmus test. If you are capable of listening to them, the stalls can direct you as well as any great maestro could, but no good will come from allowing yourself to be flattered or carried away, for the audi-ence can then become like a wild horse out to unsaddle you.

Personally, I have never attended any school or academy, except for painting . . . but I have had many masters, some in spite of themselves. I firmly believe that the problem is not so much accepting teaching, as assimilating the trade from masters. It is by 'cohabiting' with the master that the pupil 'grasps': he does not 'learn', but 'thieves' the trade.

How does one teach the actor's art?

As in every profession, the master, if you follow him with great attention, will reveal his secrets, and if you succeed in making them yours, well and good ... otherwise, there's nothing to be done. I certainly have thieved shamelessly, in the first place from the story-tellers on the lake, who imparted their lessons with a lightness of touch and without appearing to do so. The *mezarat* fable-tellers always taught me to be patient and open with beginners.

And so I today teach my pupils in the style of a conjurer who shows every time how his tricks are done, including the difference between gesturing and gesticulating. Gesticulating means movement without control, at random. The art of the gesture, on the contrary, implies great control of your own ges-tures, total awareness of the movement of each limb, from hands to chest, to feet, all with great economy and harmony.

I did not find it easy to acquire agility and speed of reflex on stage. I have had as masters in mime such figures as Jacques Lecoq and Etienne Decroux, but I have to admit that I came to these masters with invaluable previous training thanks to the numerous punch-ups in which I was often involved with boys of my own age at the lakeside. Boxing matches, brawls, kick-ings and knees to the groin were the order of the day in the Valtravaglia.

I came from a quiet town where displays of strength and aggression were very rare, but when I got to Porto I found myself battered about by those uncouth ruffians. Being shy and completely without any aggressive inclination, I invariably ended up on the ground, covered in bruises.

'When are you going to stop letting yourself be beaten about like a mattress?' Knocked black and blue by all and sundry, especially by Manassa and Mangina, I found myself, to make matters worse, mocked and reproached by my father. 'Learn to stick up for yourself! Do you want me coming along to protect you, as though you were some little girl with a runny nose? Get off your backside and learn how to dodge blows, to block punches and look after yourself.' 'And who's going to teach me?' 'If you go to Luino, there's a boxing school.'

I went along. 'What are you doing here?' 'I want to train!' When I took off my coat and stood there all puny and lanky, the trainer burst out laughing uproariously. He nearly wet himself. 'Come and see the next boxing champion! Away you go and present yourself to the fencing class. Maybe they'll take you on. It might help make you a bit more agile . . . and learn at least how to get out of the way of punches.'

But alas! the rapier and sword-fencing classes were full.

They took me on for the sabre course, mainly I think to make up the numbers. It was not a very successful course, indeed there were only four people on it. The sabre master was of Sicilian origin, and would not hear of us using 'irons' in the first months; nothing but bare hands. 'Duelling is an affair requiring cut and thrust by the hand, the arm, the chest, the hips and legs, and above all the brain. The sword will be the extension of the hand. You must learn all the positions by heart so that you can execute them with your eyes shut.'

After a couple of months of that discipline, like a gun-slinger exiting from a saloon, I presented myself at the quayside, the invariable arena for encounters, and there I had my first live match with Manassa. He squared up in the boxer's 'classical upright position' while I came forward in the pose of the swordsman: left arm behind back, chest out, right arm outstretched, hand with fingers straight, tightly together and rigid as a blade. Lunge . . . parry . . . feint . . . straight thrust . . . whack! A blow to Manassa's face, causing him to wrinkle his nose in disbelief. 'For Christ's sake! That's not fair! What kind of boxing is that?'

A crowd of boys and one or two older fishermen had gathered round the two fighters. Manassa returned to the fray, throwing a couple of rapid punches, but with such fury that he knocked himself off-balance. I kept my poise, like a skilled swordsman. I moved back with swift steps without letting my outstretched arm fall, waving it about at any attack from Manassa. Swerve . . . feint . . . sideways parry . . . draw back . . . lunge . . . whack! One more blow to the boxer's body . . . further delivery of downward stroke . . . Manassa on the ground, nose, forehead and cheek bones bright red. 'Oh no, bloody hell! This is piss-awful boxing,' he snorted. 'I've had it up to here . . . it's not fair!'

'Quite fair,' intoned Mangina, in the authoritative tones of a Boxing Board of Control umpire. 'Everyone is entitled to fight in the style he chooses, so long as he fights with his bare hands. No sticks or stones. If someone prefers to strike out with only one hand, it's up to him, no complaints. It's a style like any other. The classic, one-armed style!' And from that day on, they gave me the name 'the cripple', but with high respect.

But I couldn't abide that nickname, and had to do something about it. I decided to learn to fight with both hands . . . still in the manner of a fencer, but swinging both arms as though I were holding several sabres. I practised every day with my brother, who acted as my trainer. To block my assaults, Fulvio started to kick out wildly. Without realising it, we had reinvented a kind of exotic, perhaps Chinese, boxing. To be able to strike better with the feet, we wheeled round continually this way and that, kicking out without warning, and at the same time throwing punches and even head-butting. Finally they changed my nickname: I became the 'spinning-top', which was hardly a great improvement!

# CHAPTER 10

## *African War and World War*

In 1935, the African war broke out. Universal delight: Italy was invading Abyssinia!

'We are going there to colonise, not to pillage,' they taught us, 'we're there to build bridges, dams and roads, to bring civilisation to those savages. As a bonus, Italy will become an empire.' I could not understand why my father was cursing and swearing and muttering to himself about 'bare-faced robbery'. 'Even the beggars want their place in the sun. To knock at Europe's door and get them to open it for us, we have to go shooting people in Africa. A fine way to win the respect of the plutocrat bosses of this world!'

At school they told us: 'We will revenge the massacres of Macallé and Adua. The Abyssinian slaves of the Negus will be liberated!'

Pa' Fo exploded, striving to keep his voice down: 'Sure thing, and to liberate them more quickly, they'll gas them!' My mother nodded, adding: 'You can bet on it.' I stared at my parents in disbelief, thinking to myself: 'What a dreadful family of anti-Italian defeatists!' How could an honest and courageous man like my father express these contemptuous sentiments towards the Duce and the fatherland? And that's before he got onto the subject of the king: 'That criminal dwarf!' were his insulting words.

I was in awe of my father but one day I almost assaulted him as I churned out the grand words which we had learned by rote at school: the Risorgimento . . . the First World War to free Trento and Trieste . . . the heroic sacrifice of our glorious soldiers . . . the sense of patriotism . . . 'And you of all people! On your deputy station-master jacket, you show off all those medals, and you've got silver ribbons on your arm to show you were wounded . . . so why did you volunteer to fight with the Arditi?'

I expected Pa' Fo to give me a cuff on the jaw, but he didn't. He smiled, and checked me gently. 'Calm down. First of all, I did not volunteer. I was called up. I was nineteen, I was born in 1898, and I was enlisted in the infantry. After one month, I was already at the front. Can you imagine that? You were a complete innocent, and they shunted you into that hell. What could you have learned about weapons, combat or military strategy? Apart from rifles and Drapen (hand bombs, whose real name is Strapne), machine guns, mortars . . . nothing at all! You were given a mouthful of *grappa* to knock back at top speed before every attack, then they threw you forward to get yourself killed, and you were a sitting duck: skewer them or they skewer you. After the first six days on the Carso border, half of our battalion was already done for, slaughtered. On the seventh day we were relieved. I was literally a wreck. Two men from my village had been blown apart when a howitzer got them dead-centre, only five paces from where I was dug in. All that was left of those poor bastards who arrived at the same time as me were some bits of flesh and blood scattered all over the place. Everywhere there was the acrid stench of gunpowder and the sickly smell of blood and guts. And the screams of the wounded and the dying, groans and moans that would rip the skin off your body.

'Three "fresh" companies arrived to relieve us, and the survivors among us, numbed and dazed, went down to the town below, where they had set up services and lodgings behind the lines, and from there the wounded were moved to hospital. I received treatment too. I had some shrapnel in my shoulder, and they took it out just like that . . . with me standing upright, without anaesthetic . . . there was enough "sleeping portion" only for the most serious cases. They put three stitches in me and sent me on my way. It was there that I met Gigi Briasco, my cousin from Leggiuno. He had been in the army for three years, which made him a veteran. They were treating him for a "bang on the head", as the men said, in other words a bad fracture of the skull. I was going to embrace him but he held me back: "Steady, Felice! My stomach's like patchwork embroidery . . . I got a full blast of Drapen roses!"

'I waited till they patched up his head and we went down together to where they were dishing out the grub. There was a queue as far as you could see.

"Come on, let's go to the officers' mess."

"You've been promoted?"

"Of course I have. I'm a sergeant. But it's not the rank that gets me in. It's this nonsense." He had on his shoulder a gold-embroidered circle with a dagger and a bomb bursting into flames.

"What's that?"

"It's the emblem of the *Arditi.*"

"Did you join up with that lot?" I asked incredulously.

"Yes, third company, *Arditi* battalion. It's the only way to save your hide."

"You must be kidding. What do you mean? Don't tell me you've got yourself an easy number."

"No way. I'm still risking my skin. It's my job to go over the top at night-time, in the open, snip through the barbed wire, defuse the mines the Krauts have been planting left, right and centre . . . in other words, clear the ground our lads will have to cross the next day when they launch the attack. But once we've done our work, we crawl back into the trenches and get sent back to a base away from the front . . . those of us that have made it back, obviously."

"Exactly, and how many would that be? How many manage not to get shot by snipers, blown up by booby traps or caught by machine gun fire when flares leave them exposed?"

"This is true," my cousin admitted, "but tell me something, Felice. Am I right in saying that less than half of your company is still alive after six days here? Now take my lot. There are one hundred and twenty of us in all, of whom around fifteen copped it in the last three months, and we've taken part in about twenty operations. Do your own sums and you'll see the advantages: there's no doubt that what we're doing in the *Arditi* will give you pains in the balls like nothing you've ever felt . . . every time you get back from an operation, you've got an ache in your arse that stops you doing a shit for three days . . . things sticking out of you . . . bits of wire that ripped your skin . . . but it still all adds up in our favour. We're going to make it home with our hide intact, some more intact than others, but for you lot, the poor bloody infantry, it's worse than being on a shooting range in a fairground . . . three balls a penny! So far, it's gone OK for you, Felice, but it's not exactly easy to pull out the winning ball in the raffle every time. It's like being in a casino . . . look at it any way you like, the banker always wins in the end. The croupiers are the generals, the owners of the casinos are the king and the man-ufacturers of the transports, cannons and bombs. They're the ones who spin the wheel and they're playing with our lives. Get smart, raise the stakes if you want to bugger death."

'So that was it. My cousin Briasco had convinced me. The very next day, I went off to join up with the *Arditi*. Panic attacks, crawling about like a lizard, holes all over my body, but I made it. Unfortunately the right number in the raffle didn't come up for cousin Briasco, and he was left there. My mother's sister received a solemn encomium and a silver medal, but they never brought his body back.'

I was deeply moved by my father's story, and stayed silent for a while, then said: 'But tell me, Papà, why do you still wear all these decorations on your jacket?'

'They're trinkets, but they're like lightning conductors. It's thanks to them that I haven't been reported or suspended, and even that I escaped arrest a couple of times. In my line of work, I come across any number of high and mighty Fascists who are fanatical about this goddam regime, and who drone drearily on about the "glory of the faith and the ideal". I don't suffer fools gladly, and every time I end up sniggering at them. So what do I get from them? "Mind your tongue, or I'll report you." "Come on you bunch of wankers," I tell them, "want to report these as well?" and I puff my chest full out and shove my collection of honours, including the *Arditi* badge and the solemn encomium, in their face! Once I dropped my trousers in front of a blustering Fascist lady to show her my injured leg and silver knee-cap, and even gave her the Fascist war cry – *Eia, Eia, Alalà*! Who do you think's going to take the chance of dragging a haul of trophies like that before a court?'

At which point, I started laughing out loud.

From that day on, every time someone came to our school to recite a eulogy to the regime or to deliver a panegyric on the sacred martyrs of the fatherland, I could not help seeing my father on the platform, his trousers around his ankles, jumping from one foot to the other, showing off his wounds and his silvery knee. He does not wear underpants . . . his privates are adorned with a garland of merrily ringing medals.

It often happened in class that the teacher or someone else would interrupt the talk and yell at me in a highly outraged tone: 'You, boy . . . what do you mean by that idiot grin?'

'No, sir,' I would reply, lying through my teeth, 'it is not a grin. I was just trying to hold back the emotion!'

# CHAPTER II

## *The Mystery of the Amorous Statues*

A beautiful eighteenth-century villa, surrounded by a park with a river on one side, stood facing the lake on the outskirts of the town. Here and there stood clumps of woodland – oaks, silver firs and beeches. Statues in the Palladian style depicting nymphs, satyrs and various gods had been placed among the trees to give a spurious impression of randomness. In the villa lived the owners of the glassworks. The park was enclosed by a long fence around the entire perimeter.

The keeper in charge of the life of the trees was called Serene, surname Weather. His brother's name was Cloudy, indisputable proof of the madness of the town. He was a registered gardener with all his diplomas in order and had previously worked on the Borromeo family's island, the Isola Madre. He was a quiet man, but he too one day went mad and was carried off in the usual padded van to the mental hospital in Varese. The fault lay with a passionate love affair which had broken out among the statues in the park. Absurd? A pataphysical hyperbole? It may be, but for Serene, who had no idea what pataphysics were, it was a tragic business all the same.

I was fond of that gardener so, once a few weeks had passed, I went to visit him in the hospital in Varese together with Giuda and Tajabis, two friends who were both a bit older than me. Serene seemed tranquil enough, as would be expected of someone of that name, and appeared both very happy to see us and keen to confide in us about what had caused him to lose his mind. In the visiting room, he started talking: 'It all began with the creepers growing so wild and thick over the statues in the park that you could hardly make them out. The owner ordered me: "You'll have to get rid of those creepers, otherwise they're going to break the statues to pieces."

'Armed with scythe, secateurs and saw, I started to clear the creepers away, but gently because you have to be careful not to scratch their skin. Among the statues, there were some copies of Roman originals, but there were so many branches and leaves over them that it was impossible to make out if they were male or female. I started hacking away at the shrubbery at the base, and the feet were the first to emerge. It's hard to tell the sex of a statue from its feet. Working my way up, I liberated the legs . . . long . . . delicately carved . . . certainly female . . . or maybe Apollo, which is more or less the same . . . the only difference is at the join in the legs, and the lyre.

'And in fact it was him, the god of music, with his outsized guitar. Stark naked, except for a strategically placed loincloth . . . although it was not much good, since you could still make out his thingummy in its entirety . . . small and discreet. The gods never need to overdo things.

'The second statue I set to work on was a female. Beautiful she was, pushing up through wisteria and trailing plants. Snip, snip, and legs like columns appear . . . pubic region . . . thighs . . . buttocks . . . magnificent! Carrying on up, the stomach and tits emerged. My hands were shaking as I revealed those two lovely curves. She seemed to be breathing. Finally the neck and face, mouth and eyes began to peep out . . . she smiled and looked at me . . . at me! . . . as if to say "Thank you for rescuing me!"

'So I said to myself, am I mad? What's come over me? I felt I wanted to caress her all over, and I ran my fingers and hands over those cheeks of hers, so soft as to make me go all fluttery. Who knows what goddess she was? Perhaps she was a nymph . . . yes, she must be a nymph.

'I was standing there in a state of enchantment when my eyes happened to drift over to the right and I saw Apollo staring at me, or more precisely gazing at the nymph. What's going on? I hadn't even noticed that his face was turned in this direction. I went up to him, took a look at the join of the neck and touched it. It was warm, in fact it was burning as though the stone had been twisted. Must be because of the friction with the branches which I had just cleared away. I look back over at the nymph; she had one hand over her breasts . . . and she seems to have turned away a little, as though she were embarrassed at the too intrusive stare from Apollo. Come on! That's enough! I'm going off my head. This is turning into a nightmare. Time to get on with freeing the next sculpture, the third.

'It's much easier now. I know how to go about it. I clear away creepers as though shearing sheep. Here we go, torso emerging . . . another male . . . but this time there's an animal tail . . . it's all tangled, as you would expect if you found a statue under layers of ivy and fungus. There's no way of knowing what kind of posture it was supposed to have . . . Ah! Got it! Once I clear away the bulk of the branches, a quadruped emerges. Is it a man on horseback? No, it's a centaur.

'Muscles taut and tense, a fine chest, and underneath the hindquarters, a grand piece of equipment . . . proud and erect . . . horses have no sense of measure. In addition, this quadruped is holding a bow with an arrow ready for firing, the whole structure set in bronze. As though by chance, the nymph turned to face the centaur, and the look of the man on horseback seemed fixed on the woman's eyes. Statuesque love at first sight? I'm going off my head.

'It's getting dark. I go home, but I'm back the following morning. God in heaven, no sign of the centaur! On the ground nearby there's only the quiver with two arrows . . . nothing else. Want to bet someone has stolen it? There's a furrow on the grass, as though someone has dragged it along the ground. I follow the track and it leads me to the stables . . . door wide open . . . horses missing . . . I look around. Thank God, they're all down there drinking at the pond. I go to round them up. Sweet Christ, there's one in the water, drowned. Where did all that blood come from? A headless horse? No, it's the centaur decapitated!

'I trip over something . . . what's my axe doing here? I hear someone shouting. It's Signora Lazarini calling for me. Her voice comes from over beside the statues. I go running down and see the master beside her. They are extremely upset. The Apollo is lying on the ground with a bronze arrow stuck in his chest. The statue of the nymph is still upright but her arms are raised in the air in a gesture of despair and triumph, and in her left hand, she is holding an arrow.

' "Who is responsible for this disaster?" The Signora's tone is menacing. "Whose iron club is this?" She picks it off the ground, extracting it from Apollo's tightly locked fingers. "Don't tell me it's part of the statue. Apollo with a club!"

' "No, the club is mine, Signora, and so is the axe which has smashed the centaur in two. But I know nothing about it . . . and don't ask me what she's doing, the nymph I mean, with a bow in her hand. And I don't know why she has her arms in the air either, because earlier on they were down at her sides, I'm sure of that. And she had one hand over her breasts, turned slightly this way . . . yes, there's no doubt about it, somebody moved them during the night. These sculptures couldn't have moved by themselves. Who put the bow in the nymph's hand? It belonged to the centaur who is now at the bottom of the lake with no head."

'The master and his lady stared at me incredulously, then bombarded me with questions. "Excuse me if I make so bold, but in my view a real tragedy has occurred. I had noticed right away how they stared at each other, her and him . . . the half-horse . . . with real lust! And above all, you should have seen the miserable face that Apollo had on him . . . glowering like nothing so much as a statue of jealousy! I could swear it, it was him, Apollo, who smashed the centaur, and then the nymph, beside herself with jealousy, took revenge by firing arrows at him."

'The master burst out guffawing. "A tragedy of love and jealousy between statues!"

'But I say, "Don't you go believing that I'm responsible for this whole business all by myself. Apart from the fact that you'd need a tractor to drag that blessed statue of the centaur down to the lake . . . and no, I did not touch the tractor. The trunk of the centaur is on the tractor? I know nothing about it. No idea! You want to drive me crazy. So is this all some kind of joke? Not for me it isn't!"

'Insults, sniggers, threats, and it's me that ends up in the madhouse. They're off their heads, every last one of them.'

# CHAPTER 12

## *The Overhead Cable*

Like all children in this world who live in the country, we in Porto went on fruit-pilfering expeditions in orchards and farms. The point of stealing fruit was not to satisfy hunger but to test our courage in the face of the danger of having a potshot aimed at our backsides, as they do with toads. The local peasants were pitiless: if they caught you making off with their fruit, they fired at you with rifles loaded with salt . . . and it was painful!

My brother Fulvio and I were part of a gang where an obligatory rite of passage was risking your neck, whether by diving head-first into the lake from the rock face in the Caldé quarry, or by taking suicide runs on the trolleys which sped along the railway lines down to the loading point for the abandoned furnaces . . .

The craziest thing we got up to was undoubtedly speeding along the overhead cable constructed for moving bundles of wood down from the uplands: an iron or copper cable was put up by the wood-cutters to run from the Corveggio Alps, at a height of eight hundred metres, down to the ramps in Tramezzo. The tree trunks and bundles of timber were attached to rollers which rattled down the cable and crashed into enormous buffers at the foot . . . the impact was to say the least violent!

The first one to suspend himself from the rollers was Manàch, the son of a wood-cutter. With one hand he grabbed hold of a steel hook and with the other he gripped one of the runners and off he went as though it were the easiest thing in the world.

All the rest of us were down in the valley looking up, holding our breath, in suspended animation, our eyes clouding over. He came down at top speed. When he got close to the buffers at the bottom, he tried to slow down . . . Good Lord, he's going to crash into the wooden planks, he's going to be jelly! But Manàch knew what he was doing and tightened his grip on the steel hook to make it act as a brake . . . now he's hanging on to that alone. The friction on the wire is giving off as many sparks as a soldering iron. Bloody hell! He's not slowing down enough. He'll be pulped!

No, look, he's braking. He's still at speed when he gets to the buffers but there is no crash. Our whizzing hero throws his legs in the air to soften the blow while, as pale as shadows, we all let out a yell. I fall full length to the ground. 'Now it's the turn of you lot,' sneers Manàch.

We do our calculations. First off should be Bigulòt, son of a fisherman. He chooses a less steep and risky descent. He makes it! He wobbles a bit . . . shaves the top of a few chestnuts trees, takes a couple of whiplash blows in the face but holds on . . . the final bang is not too bad.

The boy ahead of me starts off well but halfway down scrapes along the top of a gigantic, very high elm tree. He did not have the strength to raise his legs and body, so gets into a tangle with the foliage but holds on and comes through, but when he gets to the destination, he is covered in cuts and scratches: face, arms and legs all bleeding. A dip in the stream, and he's as right as rain.

Now it's my turn and I am just a little anxious. In compari-son with those fearless spirits, I feel like a wet sponge but, goaded by pride, I work up my courage. I had heard Manàch and Bigulòt making sniggering remarks about my more or less non-existent chances of coming out in one piece. I had the one advantage, only one, of having been able to observe with great care all the other descents. I had noted that each one had almost instinctively used his feet, or rather his boots, to drag along the cable and reduce speed. Having mastered that detail, I tie two hooks, one for each foot, with pieces of string to the soles of my boots.

My companions observe me with a kind of cruel irony. I take hold of one of the hooks which hangs from a runner, then of another . . . I let my body go limp . . . but at once begin to sway as though I were on a trapeze until I manage to attach the hooks sticking out of my boots to the wire of the cable. My invention works marvellously. I manage to control the speed with some ease. When I want to accelerate, all I have to do is release my foot-hold: to brake, I clutch more tightly. The boys following my progress from down below give up making a fool of me.

'Oh, shitty-pants has got away with it. Good old tight-arse, you're an eagle!' they shout at me.

When I climbed down from the overhead cable, I was so excited and euphoric that I did not even notice that smoke was coming from my feet: the friction had caused the hooks to overheat and they were literally burning the soles of my boots.

When I got back home, I had a problem in explaining to Mamma how that disaster had come about: the two soles seemed to have been sawn in half.

## CHAPTER 13

## *Gog*

By doing portraits, I bought a dog. An extraordinary dog!

The idea of marketing myself as a portrait-painter had come to me in the last year of primary school while doing a drawing of my teacher. She was a youngish woman with a delicate face in which her almost almond-shaped eyes, thin nose and prominent lips stood out. Her neck was long, almost exaggeratedly so. I was very fond of her. When five years later I came across Modigliani's portraits at the Brera Academy, I exclaimed: 'Oh, he must have known my primary-school teacher!'

That first portrait brought me some success, and I set out to do portraits of several of my school-fellows, male and female. I acquired a reputation: more than one enthusiastic parent repaid me with gifts, some in cash. Next it was the turn of the mayor's daughters, then the whole family.

A horse-breeder who had produced flat-racing and show-jumping champions at Besnate (near the lake of the same name) sent for me. I arrived at his estate complete with my brushes, paints and Fabriano albums, to be greeted by a great pawing of hooves which made the earth tremble. On the dressage ground not less than thirty horses were galloping past at high speed. Some were ridden by a jockey, others were running riderless in a pack. The breeder was very busy and did not even say hello. A girl of more or less my age, all ringlets and curls, who looked like Shirley Temple, came over to me: her name was Ornella. She then introduced Matilde, her elder sister, a mass of blonde curls: splendid! To top it all, three other sisters appeared, a total of five who, seen together, looked like the chorus of angels in a Benozzo Gozzoli painting.

Ornella introduced them one by one. I was worried and asked if they wanted me to paint them all: 'Yes,' they replied in unison. 'In order of age,' added Ornella. 'I am the youngest, so it's my turn first.'

'Don't worry. We don't expect you to paint us all in the same day!' continued Ornella. 'You can take until tomorrow, working through the night if you need to!' With that, they burst out laughing all together.

To cut a long story short, I began by doing a sketch of Ornella's face. Never had I felt so insecure. The pencil had none of its normal fluency; it seemed to stutter . . . I had to rub out, start again . . . then towards the end, when adding the colour, I started to get to grips with the whole thing. I heard exclamations of amazement behind me. I had succeeded, but I was literally soaking with sweat. When I completed the first portrait, I realised that the breeder was standing among the onlookers. 'Not bad,' was his comment, 'very promising! If you were a colt, I would say it was worthwhile giving you a run-out on the track and keeping an eye on you!' Not all five portraits came out as I would have wished, but Gozzoli's angel chorus was quite satisfied.

The breeder, to let me stretch my legs and brain, took me to see the stables. As we moved from box to box, he pointed out his champions. On the round, we passed in front of a compound where half a dozen gigantic puppies were creating a din: they were all thoroughbred Great Danes. I was no great lover of dogs, but I was fascinated by that curious species of beast: the male moved around the compound with the elegance of an animal in a riding school. That evening, before I went home, the great horseman, his daughters gathered round him, was about to say goodbye, but with a certain embarrassment he blurted out: 'I'd like to give you something, but I've no idea what to choose. I could give you some money, but it doesn't seem a good idea. How about a paint box and an easel?' I interrupted him. 'Would one of those Great Danes cost a lot?' The breeder, who seemed to be posing for a group photograph with his whole chorus of angels, was caught on the hop. 'I'm sorry, but those animals are all already spoken for.' Then he added hurriedly, evidently fearful that he would be contradicted by his daughters: 'However, there is one, the least developed, maybe I could let you have that one . . .'

Another silence, then, like a high-pitched alleluia, the girls all came in with: 'That's it! Gog is his!'

I was jumping for joy as we went back to the kennel. 'There you are, the grey one with the white paws and the star-shaped patch on his face is Gog, and he's your very own!'

'Papà says he is the worst of the pack, but it's not true. It's just that he's a bit shy compared to the others, who are a gang of delinquents!'

I took my 'beast' home with me that very evening. Gog is the name of one of the two monsters of the Apocalypse, Gog and Magog, but my Great Dane puppy had none of the all-devouring ferocity of the biblical myth. On the contrary, he was the most gentle and timorous creature I had ever come across. He cowered under the seat in the train compartment, and to get him off I had to take him in my arms. He weighed more than me.

When I got home, Fulvio and Bianca screamed with delight, and the cat, a she-cat, sniffed at him and from the odour he was emanating, understood at once that she was facing a big, harmless bundle of terror. Mamma instantly took to him and smothered him with caresses.

Gog was continually in the company of my brother, my sister and myself, as well as of the other children in our gang, whether we were in the piazza or in the woods. He came with us when we went on fruit-stealing expeditions, and was the first to skedaddle . . . all it took was the sound of a dog barking from the haystack. He was literally terrified of Alsatians, or of any kind of mongrel which gave him a menacing growl . . . you would immediately see him make off, his tail between his legs, scraping along the walls.

That was when he was a puppy . . . but within a couple of months he had grown under our very eyes. He developed a leopard's chest, paws, buttocks, neck – his whole body was enriched by the muscle structure of a powerful Great Dane, but his expression and demeanour remained the same as Walt Disney's Pluto: puzzled and dazzled. For this reason we had no hesitation in letting him roam freely anywhere he wanted: there was no danger. He wandered around the town and into the villages in the valley. Everyone recognised him and knew that he was as meek as an angel. They called him over, fed him titbits, hugged him. The children jumped on his back as though he were a horse, and Gog put up with it all.

The only drawback was his excessive appetite: he wolfed huge bowls of meaty stew, but by the first belch the meal was already digested. As soon as we sat down to table, he would come up to beg for left-overs, and there was no way of shooing him off. Pa' Fo did not want him 'slobbering away' between his feet. After a few months, all of a sudden he gave up begging. Had he learned some dignity? Not a bit of it: he had taken to stealing chickens.

Near our house, there were chicken runs in the orchards and farms. For a giant hound like ours it was child's play to leap over wire netting around any compound: one bound, a snatch at a cockerel or chicken, and off he would race . . . four bites, and flesh, bones and even feathers were gone. I have no idea why, but he did respect the hen run in our garden, but no others. A quarter of an hour later without fail, the owners of the pillaged cages were at our door. We did not even allow them to finish their complaints. 'Just go into our garden. Go over to the compound and help yourselves to any hen or cock-erel you like, and accept our apologies!' By now there was a ban in our house against eating fowl, since we needed them all to recompense the people whose poultry had provided Gog with a snack.

Soon, apart from the chicken, geese and turkeys, even the dogs, including the large hounds, got out of the way when he came along. I once saw a boxer terrier attempt to attack him and end up bleeding at the bottom of a ditch.

Three years passed, I enrolled at the Brera Academy and had to get the train every morning for Milan. Gog came with me to the station and was there punctually each evening to meet me. He did everything by himself, and if he did not see me on the first evening train, he came back to meet me off the later one. He had learned the railway timetable.

A few years later, the three children in the family had to move to Milan to continue our education. Mamma came with us, but Pa' Fo went back to take charge of the station at Pino Tronzano. Gog was briefly pensioned off in a dog home in the open countryside, run by a person we trusted. In that home, the dogs were almost always allowed out in the fresh air and only locked up at night-time, but Gog could not get used to that routine. After a few days, he rebelled against his keeper who, with a large stick, tried to convince him to go back to his place in the cage. The Great Dane pounced on him, exactly like the mythical monster in the Bible. The man only just managed to free himself and open the gates. Gog exited without a sound and made off for the woods.

When we returned to the lake that Sunday, we learned of the dog's escape and learned also that he had attacked lambs in various parts of the valley. Together with my brother, I travelled throughout the countryside asking the peasants for news of the dog. Many of them knew us: 'They caught sight of him near Muceno. They say he has become the leader of a pack of wild dogs. The peasants in Cerasa, Masnago and Tramezzo are getting together under the direction of the *carabinieri* to hunt him down.'

We went up to Domo and spoke to the parish priest, but when he found out that Gog was our dog, he turned offensive: 'You scum, bunch of rogues! What do you think you're doing letting a beast like that loose? It's worse than a panther. It's got together with a pack of mongrels: they're slaughtering calves and devouring them on the spot.'

His philippic was interrupted by a series of shots. 'Can that be the hunters?' asked Fulvio. 'Certainly, and you can be sure they're not shooting quails or sparrows. It's not the season.' We ran in the direction of the shots. We reached the pathway, and there on a rise in the ground stood the hunters with their rifles.

Further on, by the side of a stream, lay a lamb with its intestines hanging out. A little further on, in the shallows, lay two or three large dogs. One of them, lying belly up, was Gog.

# CHAPTER 14

## *The Engineer-Count*

Glass-blowers, fishers, mechanics and smugglers were not the only inhabitants of the Valtravaglia; families of wealthy people lived there too and they had villas, gardens and woodland which snuggled close to the mountain, and palaces which lined the coast from Caldè to Magadino.

A nobleman, Count Mangelli, whom everyone in his firm addressed as 'Engineer', could often be seen around the streets of Porto.

He always moved with elegance, body upright, looking people straight in the face even if he gave the impression of not really seeing them. He responded with a nod of the head to anyone who greeted him but never stopped, not even when people called out to him or asked after his health. He was badly shaven, did not look exactly dirty but wore a shirt of indefinite colour under an old jacket. The melancholy of his expression was deeply affecting.

The tragedy which had reduced him to this state had occurred at the Heremitage Hotel, the most celebrated and luxurious of the whole coastline. Everyone who was anyone in the valley had gathered for one of the customary receptions in honour of someone or other. There were beautiful women there, but none more so than Sveva Rosmini, the Engineer's wife. Everyone in those circles knew about the affair between

Signora Sveva and Signor Colussi, a lawyer who was also managing director of FIVEC (International Glass and Crystal
Company). In the course of the party, Signora Sveva got up
from her table, and, hips swaying like a model, made her way
resolutely towards the back of the hall, where her lover was
seated.

The young, highly attractive, dark-skinned daughter of
Dr Grillo, the local general practitioner, was at the same table,
and it was clear to everyone that Colussi was courting her
without subtlety or concealment. For the whole evening, young
Grillo had demonstrated by a laughter which resembled the
clucking of an excited hen her contented delight at the lawyer's
repeated fondling of her backside. Signora Sveva had put up
with this throughout the whole dinner, from the entrée to the
main course, but when the fish was produced, she marched up
to the table of the flirtatious twosome, picked up from the
platter a large boiled trout garnished with mayonnaise, and
swung it in the air before bringing it smartly down on the face
of the terrified, still clucking, young lady. The trout itself broke
in two but Signora Sveva, brandishing the body of the fish by
the tail, rammed it with a masterly flourish into the open
mouth of the faithless lawyer. Mayhem ensued. The recently-
fondled young lady fainted, face-down, on a delicately cooked
perch. The lawyer, after a moment's initial hesitation, gave the
Signora a slap. She responded by throwing herself into his arms.
A voice rang out, 'Musica, maestro!' and in an instant the orchestra struck up a festive polka. The dancefloor filled with dancing
couples, and even the lawyer and his mistress took to the floor,
but from the movement of their bodies it was clear that their
refrain was 'You, rascal you.' At the termination of a whirl, he
seized her by the hem of her dress, ripping it neatly apart. The

Signora, resplendent in knickers and suspender belt, let out a scream, to general applause and appreciation for those beguiling thighs and heaving breasts. Signora Sveva *desnuda* jumped onto the lawyer at about the level of his kidneys: 'Tally ho, stallion, show me what you're made of!' Although no one had noticed, Signora Sveva's husband, the Engineer, had come on the scene a few moments previously. Some of the more giddy diners gave him a slap on the back as a sign of jovial fellow feeling.

All of sudden, everyone froze. The horsewoman stopped in her tracks for one moment, then: 'What are you doing there, my dear? Don't look so aghast! Get a filly and do a lap yourself.' So saying, she dug her knees into her lover's kidneys and off she galloped, shrieking like a horserider from the Maremma. Other excited ladies jumped onto the backs of their own cavaliers. At that moment, the daughter, still under the weather, came in, leaning on her father. The Engineer remained stock-still, as though he were somewhere else.

Only when the great gallop was over did people notice that the Count had exited. For two days there was no trace of him. 'He'll have gone to Milan, or to his brother's in Switzerland,' was the relaxed comment of his wife. But no one had seen him get on a train or buy a ticket. 'He's not touched the car,' observed their daughter, 'it's still there in the garage.' Each one had his own conjectures: 'He couldn't have thrown himself into the lake, maybe from one of the high rocks?' 'The water in these parts is too cold for his tastes. Anyway, he's got no head for heights.'

In fact, there was someone who knew in detail what was going on, but he said nothing. In any case, it never crossed anyone's mind to ask him: he was Menghissu, a tramp with a constantly smiling expression. He had fought in the African war, and for more than a year had been a prisoner of the Abyssinians. He knew exactly the place where the Engineer had taken refuge, for the simple reason that he was a guest in one of his properties, a little construction with a door and one window, half-excavated in the rocks under the kilns. Unquestionably the Engineer, always perfectly mannered, would have asked Menghissu, the owner of that hovel for years even if he had never actually lived in it, for permission to take up residence.

That Sunday the people of the Valtravaglia were gathered in church to hear mass, the well-heeled and better-off in their family pews, the others in any place they could find. It was nearly midday when the choir door was flung open and the Engineer entered gingerly; he took his place in a corner of the apse behind the group of choristers, of which I was a member. He was done up in a somewhat unconventional style: on his head he had a red fez from which a golden charm was suspended. He was wearing a kind of embroidered waistcoat, but from the shoulders down he was wrapped in a large, white-woollen cloak with dangling pendants. Beneath the cloak, the observer could make out a pair of short, Turkish-style, riding breeches . . . all that was lacking was the camel. He removed his fez and bowed ever so slightly. At first a deadly silence fell on the place, followed by subdued murmuring. Everyone was staring at that face with its solemn, absent expression on top of the clownish outfit, while at the same time peeping out of the corner of one eye for the reaction of Signora Sveva, her daughter and the lawyer. At the *De profundis*, the three bent over and, trying hard not to make themselves unduly noticed, made for the exit. The chorus fell silent for one moment. The Signora tripped and uttered a somewhat rude imprecation. The chorus started up again with a crescendo of great solemnity. The Engineer-caliph slipped out by the door which leads to the sacristy.

'*Gloriam Patris laudamus,*' the choir ended.

When mass was over, I returned to the sacristy with the other choristers. Each one of us busied himself, removing his white surplice and red soutane and hanging them up in the wardrobe. My peg was in the corridor which led to the bell-tower. The sacristan accosted me and asked me: 'Dario, would you mind going up there a moment and finding out what has been going on? I think the bell ropes must have got twisted . . . the bells won't ring any more!'

No sooner said than done. I climb up the staircase: three flights of stairs, three landings, and there I am at the turrets. As I emerge in between the clockwork, I stop in terror: there, stretched out on the bell's crosspiece, is the Engineer wrapped in his caliph-bedouin cloak. 'Is he dead?' I wonder aloud. 'No, not yet, thank you very much,' he replies in a gentlemanly way, raising his hat. Then he recognises me and adds: 'You're the station-master's son, aren't you? I heard you sing, you've got a fine contralto timbre to your voice . . . the same part I used to have when I was a choirboy.' I stutter out, awkwardly: 'I'm glad to hear it. I was sent up because the bells won't ring any more.'

'I do apologise. It was me that got the ropes tangled up. I needed some sleep and with the racket these four bells make . . . you understand . . . but relax, I'll get out of the way. I'll untangle the bells and go down.' So saying, he smiled at me and patted me on the head. It was the first time I had found in him an attitude of such cordiality.

From that day on, I often had occasion to see him. I would run into him by the lakeside, leaning over the railing at the quay or sitting on the harbour wall. Often I would catch sight of him on the Romanesque belfry of the main church in the town.

More than a month went by after the scandal at the Heremitage. Signora Sveva and her daughter Alfa began to get worried. The Engineer, who was in charge of technical operations at the glassworks, had walked off without asking for leave of absence, much less severance pay. The Signora went along to the works office to ask for some settlement, at least as regards salary: 'Very sorry, Signora, but without the authorising signature of your husband, we cannot pay out a penny.'

Sveva Rosmini gave vent to a loud curse . . . in French of course. She then went over to the executive offices of the glassworks in the company of her daughter, and burst into her lover's studio. 'Are you going to tell me what we're playing at here? They've got me on a cleft stick. The bank account's blocked, the salary frozen . . . the whole village sniggers when they see me, and you won't lift a finger to get me out of this mess!'

'Well, there might be one way for you to get complete satisfaction . . . in fact more than one,' said Colussi to calm her down. 'If you kill him, everything would get a bit more tricky, so I'd suggest you settle down and wait. Considering the unhealthiness of the place where he is lodging, the dangerous company he's keeping, the ruinous diet he's eating . . . everything points to the likelihood that your husband won't be troubling us much longer. However, the really sneaky solution would be to have him certified as insane, but to succeed you'd need to demonstrate he's no longer capable of understanding or knowing what he wants.'

Signora Sveva and her daughter had already calmed down. All they had to do was wait patiently, but regrettably the

Engineer, apart from taking to roosting in the occasional tree, turning up on the odd church tower, giving nods by way of greeting to the townspeople whom he passed and exhibiting himself in exotic clothes, gave no sign of obvious madness. In addition, the odd innocuous extravagance in a town of madmen like Porto Valtravaglia did not arouse any special surprise. However, a faint hope was dawning.

During the funeral of Jean Bartieux, founding father of the crystal works, a curious incident took place. Butrisa, the lead drummer, who for years had carried his bass drum on his back on the occasion of parades or processions, all of a sudden collapsed, keeling over with his drum. Several of the workers who had been with the firm since its foundation were there with members of their families following the hearse. The leader of the band turned to the bystanders for help. 'Is there anyone who could give a hand and take his place?' Without hesitation, the Engineer, in his caliph outfit, fez on head, pushed forward and, without so much as a by-your-leave, heaved the big bass drum onto his back. The drummer boy strapped him in. The Engineer took his place alongside the tambourines and the band took up where it had left off with the funeral march.

The following Sunday as they entered church, the people found the Engineer sitting on one of the choir stools. He was wearing a white lace surplice and one of those red soutanes which had been hanging in the wardrobe in the vestibule. So there he was, right next to me . . . and still with the fez on his head. The parish priest could not help noticing him as he came in, and stopped for a moment in bewilderment. The Count-choirboy gave him a peremptory nod whose meaning was: mind your own business and get on with the rituals!

The priest began celebrating mass. We in the choir began intoning the *Nunc Dimittis Domine*. The Engineer drew a long breath then joined decisively in the chant with a deep baritone descant. People craned their necks to get a better glimpse of the new singer. Some were even moved to applaud. Signora Sveva covered her eyes with her hands, whispering: 'Go on, go on, you're doing fine.' Her daughter Alfa sobbed: 'He's doing it deliberately to mortify us, to fuck things up for us in front of everybody.' The lawyer Colussi reproached her: 'Watch your language, especially in front of your mother!'

'I'm sorry, I forgot that "fuck up" comes from "fuck" and that certain allusions sound irreverent in this family.' Her mother shut her up with a smart slap on the mouth. As the slap rang out, the whole church turned to stare. The choir launched into the *Laudemus*.

The sacristan, holding the pole for the collection, moved among the faithful, pushing the bag attached to it in front of their faces. The Engineer appeared on the far side, he too holding a pole with a collection bag attached: he sallied forth, lance at rest, inviting the faithful to be generous. With a circular movement, he banged the bag against Colussi's nose. His first inclination was to protest, but he realised that in this situation, he'd better donate a few coins, and fast. The peremptory collecting technique did not stop there. When mass was over, the sacristan counted and recounted the cash, incredulously.

In her attempt to play the part of the despairing wife, Signora Sveva went that very evening to see Dr Ballarò, the general practitioner who also fulfilled the role of psychiatrist. It was his responsibility to issue the licence authorising the removal in the council's van for the insane of those who had gone mad.

'I'm worried about my husband,' the Signora stuttered out, amid tears. 'I'm at the end of my tether and I feel totally responsible for the crisis which has undone him. But something must be done. He's getting worse day by day.'

'I imagine that you want the Engineer to be taken to the asylum. Is that right, Signora?'

'Obviously he can't be allowed to wander around freely . . . have you heard? This morning he started singing in church.'

'You're quite right,' nodded the doctor. 'Singing during a sung mass . . . it's both blasphemous and criminal. We must have him dragged off immediately in the vehicle for the criminally insane, and with him all the choirboys, the priest, the sacristan . . . and he was out of tune into the bargain.'

'Doctor, you're not taking me seriously!'

'Look here, Signora. If you want to get your husband away from the town and its surrounds, find another solution. If I were in your shoes, I wouldn't be so obsessed with getting rid of him. I've had a long chat with the Engineer. I found him serene and relaxed. He has no resentment towards you or Colussi, no desire for revenge.'

'Oh that's wonderful, that is!' guffawed the Signora. 'No desire for revenge! You do not know my darling Count. His whole behaviour, every single outrageous thing he does, is conceived with the one intention of humiliating us, provoking us, driving us off our heads like him. Is there no one in this town who will apply the law in defence of the citizens?'

'Stop right there, Signora,' the doctor interrupted her. 'I know exactly what laws you are referring to, the same ones you were pressing the police to use – an accusation followed by summary arrest. It is my duty to warn you of one difficulty: you in your turn run the risk of a charge of unwarranted harassment of a free citizen. What are you after, Signora? Your husband doesn't get himself drunk, he's not guilty of acts of obscenity in the presence of minors, he doesn't use indecent language in a public place, doesn't spit on the ground . . . he has a job, even if only an occasional one . . .'

'A job! You're well aware he has not shown up in the offices for over a month . . .'

'I know. I'm talking of his new jobs.'

'And what would they be? Singing in church, banging the drum, taking up the collection in church or lolling about at the top of bell-towers?'

'No, no, those are only unpaid hobbies. I'm referring to his position with the sewage company.'

'Do you mean in the sewers?' She almost choked on her saliva.

'Yes, the town council is responsible for around thirty cesspits scattered throughout the valley. Your husband volunteered to take charge of the cleansing operations and to see to the maintenance of the sewage pumps.'

'So that's where that stench that he always has comes from.'

'Would you like a coffee?' he asked, to take the heat out of the situation. 'It's freshly made.'

'No, thank you. I am stuck with a sewage operator of a husband who puts on a stinking farce to cover me with shit in front of the whole town, and you lot are helping him out. You're all in it together.' She rose to her feet, issuing her parting shot as she exited. 'Bunch of shits!'

A few days later, the word got about that her daughter Alfa had run away from home. Colussi, prompted by the girl's mother, went in search of her. Good Friday was at hand. At that time, all the bells were tied up for the seven preceding days so that their ding-dong would not break the sacred silence. For the same reason, the clockwork mechanism which marked each hour with the ringing of the bells was switched off. The *mascarat-de-dolo* [the dolorous masks] roamed around the valley: these were groups of children who painted their faces red, dressed in black, waved rattles and swung bundles of ropes with which they mimed the action of scourging each other. At each crossroads, the *mascarat-de-dolo* stopped and issued warnings in the traditional manner:

'*Sem arrivà al primo quarto*'
'*El Signor l'è bastonà*'
'*Spudà*'
'*E ghe fan turment*'
'*Jesus basa i ogi e no' fa lament*'
'*Bative, bative!*'

'We have come to the first quarter'
'The Lord has been struck'
'Spat on'
'They torment him'
'Jesus, lower your eyes and make no lament'
'Beat yourselves, beat yourselves!'

With the flagellation completed, they went on their way in silence to the next crossroads, but this year the *mascarat-de-dolo* inserted a variation into the journey. They continued towards the piazza facing the Mangelli Palace, and there they stood a moment in silence until the chief penitent gave a signal, whereupon they launched into a refrain freshly composed for the occasion.

'*Vergognanza e perdisiun*'
'*Bative!*'
'*Sbatiment de dona grama, el Signor a ve condana*'
'*Fornigon*'
'*Femena bramosa scelerà, i vergogn te saran brusà*'
'*Tuti pecator smorbidi, dentra al fogo sarit rostidi!*'
'*Pentive! Pentive!*'

'Shame and perdition'
'Beat yourselves!'
'Wretched woman's embrace, the Lord will you condemn'
'Fornicators'
'Lustful, wicked woman, your loins will burn'
'All evil sinners will roast in the fire!'
'Repent! Repent!'

And off they went, miming flagellation and dancing like tarantulas on heat.

In her house, Signora Sveva put her hands over her ears, let out a scream and exploded in rage. She threw open the terrace window, came out brandishing a twin-bore hunting rifle, which she fired at the group of penitents. Two tremendous broadsides. General stampede. Two or three children rolled down the staircase, pierced by pellets from the gun.

In those years, the Stations of the Cross were still erected on the night of Good Friday. Each village was responsible for preparing one scene from *The Passion of Christ*, and the parishioners of Porto had the task of staging the so-called 'Prologue to the Passion', that is the scene featuring Herod slavering for the love of Salomè, and the subsequent beheading of Saint John the Baptist. I too was a member of the troupe, and was assigned a wonderful part – that of the slave with the fan. My job was to stand at the back and wave the huge fan so as to cool down the tyrant, his lover Herodias and the splendid Salomè, the solo dancer.

The moment the procession arrived at the town hall portico which served as the stage, four searchlights were switched on and Herod appeared embracing his lover. Herodias was played by a boy, Stralusc (which means 'arrow' in the local dialect), who, with all the necessary apparel of wig and breasts, had been dressed up as a woman. The processors took their stance around the portico, and many people came to the windows of the houses and palaces surrounding the piazza. Signora Sveva herself appeared on the terrace of the Mangelli residence.

Under the portico, the king and his concubine rolled about in a strange mime which looked more like a Graeco-Roman wrestling contest than any loving embrace. Preceded by a roll of drums, Saint John made his entrance, accusing forefinger pointed at the fornicators, to bawl out his anathema: 'Shame on your carnal lusts! Damned be the harlot!'

At this point, the guards intervened to seize hold of the recalcitrant saint and bind him to a pillar. Herodias, overcome by a hysterical crisis, smashed the plates and crystal vases (obviously all rejects from the prize-winning glassworks) noisily to the ground. *Coup de scène.* Appearance of Salomè, the dancer-daughter. The mother bursts into tears, and implores Herod: 'I beg you, cut off the head of that bastard, Saint John. He has insulted me!'

'Not on your life!' replies Herod. 'Next thing, Jesus will come along and lay on me a curse which will bugger me for all eternity.' He stops a moment, peers at the lovely Salomè and promises: 'Yeah, I will remove his head if your daughter will do a dance for me.'

Salomè is ready and willing: 'All right, I'll go along with you, but first of all, you take an oath by the Lord that as soon as the dance is over you will give the order for the saint's head to be chopped off.'

'Yes, I swear, but in return you'll have to take off all seven veils.'

'Let's make it five.'

'No, all or nothing.'

'All,' shout the guests at Herod's table, clapping their hands as they cry out.

Cue the orchestra: two accordions, one saxophone, two trumpets and the double-bass. A quiet number for starters. They strike up a languid tango. The lovely Salomè (now substituted by a girl with a stupendous body) begins her dance, all rhythmically writhing thighs and buttocks. She bends so far back that her falling hair almost scrapes along the floor. At intervals, she pulls off a veil which she tosses in the face of Saint John, who is still there, bound hand and foot.

At the third veil, Herod rises to his feet, goes over to the girl and, like an overexcited lecher, seizes hold of Salomè and hoists her onto his back. Herodias, the infuriated mother, rushes over brandishing an enormous fish by the tail. All the faithful had by now grasped the allegory and were guffawing wildly. Some scattered applause was heard, and many people turned towards the Mangelli palace to see the reaction of the lady of the house.

A few days later, Signora Sveva packed her bags and left town in a car loaded with an improbable quantity of suitcases, followed by an articulated lorry piled high with objects.

The Sunday after the great escape, the parishioners filled their church for mass as usual. We choirboys processed down the apse in our white embroidered lace surplices and red soutanes. From the foot of the nave, the Engineer made his way forward. He was dressed in jacket, neatly ironed trousers, white shirt and the usual cravat round his neck. As he passed by, one or two worshippers sniffed at him: not the remotest trace of the sewage stench. He took his seat in the family pew, smiled at the priest who returned the greeting and made a sign to us in the choir to start up with the *Te Deum Laudamus*. We began our chant, loudly: a solemn tone, which managed also to be somewhat lively, almost festive. Most of the congregation joined in what became a jubilant piece fit for any grand finale.

# CHAPTER 15

## Spawning Time

At the beginning of spring, the boys and girls along the lakeside were in a state of ferment. The *risciada*, that is, the mythical leaping of the fish from the water for their spawning festivities, was about to explode on us. For anyone unfamiliar with the reproductive conduct of ichthyological fauna, let me explain that 'spawning' indicates the moment when fish get horny. To lay their eggs, the female fish allow themselves to be carried by the waves close to the shore at the point where the waters lap the *risciada*, the rocky coast. Shortly afterwards, the male fish, after a ritual which sees them shoot out of the water and perform an infinite variety of pirouettes and dives, arrive to fertilise the eggs.

All of us children used to gather together on the quayside and there we would decide which groups to divide into and where to go. Some would choose to go northwards along the coast, and others to go down towards Laveno. Everybody brought along one or two buckets, and the more organised among us would even have fish nets or proper fishing tackle. Those in my group had chosen the beach near Luino. We agreed to meet up at dawn: it was important to be on the spot where the spawning took place before the sun rose over the mountains. We were all excited, especially the girls. As well as buckets, we brought with us long poles to chase away the snakes which would quite definitely be there, like us, on the shoreline.

The old story-tellers recounted that going along to see the fish leaping was an ancient rite dating back to the first matriarchal communities in the Verbano. Professor Civolla, acknowledged as the most prestigious historian of local traditions, insisted that as recently as one hundred years before, only girls past the age of puberty were allowed to take part in the great spawning event.

I was not even ten years old, and it was the first time I had had the chance to attend this extraordinary phenomenon. Perhaps, apart from two female classmates, I was the youngest in the gang. When we got to the shore, we started leaping about on the small gravel stones. 'Watch out! There's a grass snake!' At that, all of us turned on the poor reptile, who took to his heels, so to speak. 'There's another one . . . quick, get it!'

'But what are all these snakes after?' I asked. 'You never usually see them.'

'They're here for the same reason as us, to grab a couple of fish as soon as the spawning begins,' was the reply.

'But when does it start?'

'Hold on a minute and you'll see.'

In fact scarcely a minute later we see a ray of light fan out over the coastline under the Verzoni mountain range. The sun rises and peeps out over the highest mountain in the range, covering the whole shoreline in a golden sheen. 'Look, the bleaks are first.'

We see two or three tiny fish jump up in the air, out of water scarcely ruffled by a breath of wind, then further out, in a flash, hundreds all at once. Up, up, then splash! . . . they fall back into the water. These are males and females that spring up lightly touching each other, aquatic acrobats that lovingly brush one against the other as they somersault.

'Look, we're nearly at the mass spawn!'

The low sun, its rays piercing the air, adds glitter to the sparkle of bright scales from the thousands of excited fish. Bleaks and gudgeons by the handful begin falling on the gravel. We, jumping barefoot on the pebbles which hurt our feet, race over to the fish as they writhe about on the gravelly beach. We gather bucketfuls!

A little later, one of the older boys removed his jumper and trousers and went with his net into the water, where he was literally assaulted by acrobatic fish which flew at him and leapt into his net of their own accord. 'Quick, pass me the bucket!' Baldy, a smaller boy with a shaven head, took off all his clothes and dived into the lake in the nude, to the scandalised screams of the girls present. Soon afterwards, all the others followed his lead, wading into the middle of the foaming spray of fish now rising improbably high in the air. Then the climax: a girl stripped down to her knickers, holding her arms over her little breasts, and jumped in with the others.

'Chubs!' screamed one of her friends, as she too plunged in half-naked. 'The chubs and the whitefish are jumping as well!' And it was true: now the bigger fish were darting about, leaping in the air, twisting and turning with the agility of dolphins. The girls were now all in the water, and I too went in. I held on to my underpants to cover my embarrassment because, as I was taking them off, I had burst the elastic. In the event, no one paid any heed.

Now children and fish were leaping together in the water.

'Oh God, I'm ready for a spawning session myself,' shouted out one young lad as he dived off a rock, executing a pirouette with jack-knife entry. 'Yes, we're all up for it!' And on and on went the leaping and jumping!

By now all the buckets were filled to the brim.

'Oh help, I've got a fish in my pants!' shouted one.

'Hold on to it,' one of his friends teased him. 'It's bound to be bigger and firmer than your own tackle.' Raucous laughter all around. The girls joined in too . . . and it seemed that even the trout and pike were giggling.

'Where do we empty the buckets?' asked the curly-haired girl with the little breasts. Nearby there was a boat which had been completely sunk underwater to make the wood swell. Four or five of them hauled it off the bottom, lifted it keel-up to let the water run out, floated it upright, and then pushed and manhandled it over the bed of the lake to where we were. 'In here, jump in here, all you fishies large and small.' As though obeying orders, bleaks, chubs, ruds and trout threw themselves into the hull of the boat.

A dark-haired girl with milk-white skin, the only one endowed with regulation-size tits, cried out in anguish. 'Goodness, it's ripped my knickers!'

'Who? How? Where? When?' we all asked at the same time.

'A trout, I think. I had stuck it in there because there was no room left in my bucket.'

'Don't worry. You can have mine,' said the boy called Rosso, to reassure her.

The sun was already high in the sky when we returned, exhausted, to the quay, pushing our big boat and hanging on to its sides. Our clothes were piled up on the prow. By this time, such an atmosphere of euphoria and complicity had been created among us that each of us had long since jettisoned every residue of embarrassment. We ourselves must have resembled a merry party of spawning fish!

# CHAPTER 16

## *The Portrait of Nofret*

I had just turned thirteen. One evening as darkness was falling, we went with our gang to pinch fruit from the garden of the Polish woman whose villa was perched a hundred metres above the point where the Grifone, a cobalt-blue lake more than three hundred metres deep, widened out. We learned from Vescica, the oldest in the gang, that in those days the estate was uninhabited. I had already been to the villa at the invitation of the Polish woman's youngest son. Everything in the suite of public rooms, starting from the enormous mirrors which covered the walls and gave the impression of a fairground gallery, had seemed to me overelaborate and overdecorated.

We clambered over the precinct wall and scrambled down the creepers. The targets of the raid were the bunches of grapes hanging from the pergola which ran round almost the whole villa. There were four of us: our guide was Bigulòt, who had slipped down the wisteria onto the pergola and who was crawling along the trellises towards the most plump, juicy bunches. We followed his lead, taking care not to tumble off. I was the last in the line, with Germàn, son of a German glass-blower, crawling along ahead of me.

We were very close to the glass shutters which looked onto the Grifone when all of a sudden the central section was flung open. As one, we all crouched down among the leaves of the vine. Some people appeared at the grand windows, a man and a woman. Fortunately the darkness gave us complete cover, and from up there they could not see us. I raised my face slightly to have a look and I recognised the girl. She was called Elise and she was the woman of one of the most wealthy crooks on the entire coast – Brizzi, also known as Scorridór, a thug who was boss of the criminal underworld.

'Look at the shining ripples of the moon on the waters . . . but in this pitch black it's quite scary!' said Elise in a whisper to the man who had his arm round her waist.

The man with Elise had nothing to do with the gangsters. He was much younger. He embraced her and they kissed. Now they were talking quietly, whispering from mouth to mouth. We held our breath. I kept my face buried in the foliage and it was all I could do not to sneeze, but luckily they moved away from the window and went back inside. We heard them groaning and panting. Our fear did not permit us to take any pleasure from our peeping-tom situation. I have no idea how long their idyll of writhing, entwining and groaning went on. The lights inside the house were magnified by the mirrors which projected the images onto the windows, increasing and multiplying them so as to give the impression that there were as many as three or four couples holding tightly to each other and rolling around as though in some dance. The result was that when they closed the windows and switched off the lights, we were exhausted. We had not the strength to touch even one of those sweetly scented grapes. We dropped from the pergola and, doing our best to make as little noise as possible, climbed over the wall at an easier point further along.

When we got back to the high path hewn out in the rock-face, we walked one behind the other without speaking a word, until all of sudden Bigulòt exclaimed: 'God, they were really going at it hammer and tongs, that pair! Sometimes you could hardly tell if they were trying to screw or to claw away at each other's skin.'

'I'll tell you one thing. If Brizzi finds out, he'll skin the two of them, and no kidding!' said Vescica.

'But did you recognise the guy who was laying the girl?' I asked, awkwardly.

'Yeah, that was Stumpy, the Polish woman's eldest son.'

'Stumpy?'

'That's right, you must have seen him around. He's only got one hand. The other one got chopped off by a motorboat propeller.'

'Poor bastard. Life's hell for these rich folk!'

'Anyway,' cut in Vescica, 'I'd give one of my feet for a chance to get it off with that Elise. Wasn't she gorgeous! For one moment I saw her naked as she walked in front of the window . . . Madonna, never seen the like!'

However, of the whole gang, the one who was most over-whelmed was me. The enlarged, duplicated figures of the two lovers dancing on the window panes lingered in my brain as though from a film. Back home, I couldn't help rushing off and getting down to my painting in an attempt to capture those images of bodies moving in the lighted space. I sketched patches of colour on a black background and then repeated the same motifs on white and coloured paper. My mother asked me: 'But what's got into you? Are you off your head? That looks to me like some painting by a drunken lunatic.' And I was indeed inebriated.

The following day I was strolling along by the lake with Gog, when I heard someone call out: 'Hey, Beanpole.' It was the

127

most recent of my nicknames. I turned round and two paces away stood Stumpy, who smiled at me and said: 'They tell me you've done a raunchy portrait of my girlfriend!' My face flushed the colour of a red pepper, and I stuttered out something incomprehensible. He stopped me in my tracks: 'Take it easy. I haven't been spying on you. It's just that those mates of yours who go crawling along pergolas chatter away like the priests' housekeepers in the sacristy. Certain rumours have reached me, including a description of some of your sketches where you go into all kinds of no-holds-barred details and variations about the two of us! Would you mind letting me see them?'

'No problem!' I took him back to my house. We went up to the studio where I did my painting and I showed him my drawings and tempera sketches. He stood in silence for I don't know how long, then murmured under his breath. 'I'll buy the lot! How much do you want?' He caught me completely on the hop, and I mumbled something senseless, finally saying: 'Nothing, nothing at all . . . I'll be glad to make you a present of them,' before adding hurriedly, 'but leave me a couple of them.'

The speed with which, with only one hand, he managed to lift every one of the paintings, stare at them over and over again before tucking them all under his arm, apart from the two I had succeeded in grabbing from him, was incredible. 'You've done me a great favour,' he said as he went out, 'I don't know how to thank you.' And he rushed off down the stairs. Gog leapt up at him, trying to sink his teeth into the canvases which Stumpy was carrying off as booty.

That very evening, Manàch came racing round to my place, out of breath: 'Come out,' he screamed at me, before rushing up to meet me on the stairs. 'They've beaten up Stumpy!'

'Beaten him up? When? Where? Who was it?'

'Brizzi and his henchmen. Five of them went round to the Polish woman's house . . . they found them there, Elise and him, in bed together. They dragged her out, in the nude, and carted her off . . . she was writhing about, trying to get free, screeching like an eagle. They punched and kicked him until he was a bloody mess.'

We were interrupted by the scream of a siren. 'Hear that? They're taking him to hospital at Luino.'

The ambulance went roaring past in front of us at top speed at that very moment. It was followed by a car driven by the Polish woman, his mother.

I caught a glimpse of Elise three days later in church for Sunday mass. She was wearing dark spectacles and a scarf which covered her face up to her nose. She stayed at the back, beside the confessional. As she went out, she made me a sign to follow her. I caught up with her in the lane alongside the bell-tower. She took me by the hand. 'I have your paintings! They're lovely . . . they made me tremble all over. It was us to a tee, clasped together, in another world!'

'Thank you. How is Stum . . . I mean Rizzul . . . your boyfriend?'

'He's recovering slowly. I haven't seen him yet. His mother does not want me even to go near the hospital. She says I have been the ruination of her boy. Fortunately he sent me a card.'

'I was thinking of going to see him tomorrow.'

'Ah yes, that was why I called you over. Would you give him a letter from me?' She handed me an envelope, and gave me a hug and a kiss on the cheek. Still dazed, I was about to go when she called me back: 'Oh, I was thinking of preparing a nice surprise for my Rizzul when he gets out. Would you like to do a portrait of me?'

'Right away?'

'No, if it's possible I would come over to your house in a couple of days . . . provided your mother has no objections.'

'My mother will be delighted. See you soon.'

Almost a week went by. 'She's not coming any more . . .' I said to myself, but early one Thursday afternoon I heard a knocking at the door of my room. It was her, Elise.

'How did you get here? I was looking onto the piazza and I didn't see you cross it.'

'I came via the garden. I am being followed by Brizzi's men. Maybe this way I can give them the slip!' She took off her dark spectacles. 'Don't put this black eye in the portrait.'

She did indeed have a large, black and blue bruise. 'You're still beautiful the way you are,' I plucked up the courage to say, before blushing. I made her sit with her back to the window. 'If you don't mind, I will try to paint you against the light.'

'Do it your way . . .' Elise ran her fingers through her curls, tossing them up in the air. Her hair itself seemed to expand.

'Do you know you look exactly like an Egyptian mural painting? Look!' I opened a big book of ancient art which was lying on the table. I showed her the funeral decorations of Amenossis. 'Incredible. It could be me . . . in the nude!' She read the caption. '*Queen Nofret, wife of the Pharaoh.* Do you really think I'm as beautiful as that? You know, it could even be a great-great-grandmother, considering that my mother came from those parts. She was born at Memphis, on the Nile.' She lifted the book and kissed it: 'Ciao, welcome home, Gran!' Then she added: 'If you like, I could pose in the nude, like her!' I almost fainted on the spot. She noticed my sudden pallor and tried to fix things: 'Oh all right, if you prefer to work from memory . . . you've already seen me undressed that night at the Polish woman's house, isn't that right?'

I told her I needed to retire to the toilet a moment. I came back almost at once to find she was already posing, reclining like the Egyptian Nofret. I was extremely agitated.

The canvas was already on the easel. 'Listen, Nofret,' I said with conviction, 'I prefer to begin with a few sketches.'

I did some drawings on four sheets of paper, then began sketching on the canvas and adding colour. I was in a state of enchantment as I followed the lines of her body, so smooth in the half-light. I had no sense of passing time . . . she was still there, relaxing, as though peering onto another world.

'The sun is setting, we'll have to stop.'

Nofret shook herself as though awakening. 'Let me see what you have done,' she asked, picking up the canvas. 'Yes, yes!' and so saying she began leaping about the room. 'It's me . . . ha, ha, you've made the tresses of my hair just like the Egyptian painting.' She came over beside me. I thought she was about to kiss me but instead she lifted me off my feet, swung me around, repeating in a sing-song voice: 'Bravo, bravo . . . my little phenomenon!' She then deposited me on the couch as though I were a sack and, taking one look at her watch, exclaimed: 'Oh my God, it's seven o'clock already! I'm an hour late. That bastard Brizzi will blacken my other eye,' and off she went tripping down the stairs.

I went to the window and watched her cross the orchard with Gog at her heels. I noticed that in her haste she had forgotten her handbag. I opened the window and called to her, but she did not hear me. Not even Gog heard me, but perhaps he was only pretending not to. I grabbed hold of the bag and went racing down the stairs. I ran up the back alleys in the town, hoping to head her off before she got back to the big house where she lived with the thug. I climbed the Malarbeti staircase and came out in front of the gates which led into Brizzi's garden. There was a police car parked there. A moment later, I saw two officers coming out, pushing Brizzi in handcuffs ahead of them. Next, in a line like the Three Wise Men, emerged his henchmen, they too tightly handcuffed and chained. With them was the Neapolitan police sergeant, a friend of my father's. 'What's going on?' I asked.

'Huh, you should know,' he grinned from ear to ear, and marched down to the police van to make sure that his prisoners were properly accommodated. When the van had moved off, he turned back. Just then, Nofret and my Great Dane, who was continually rubbing up against her, made an appearance. My dog and I have the same tastes!

The girl said hello to the sergeant, who proceeded to tell both of us that the very day Stumpy was taken to hospital, the Polish woman had gone to the police to file a report against the thug and his gang for assault and serious injury to her son. As if that were not enough, the assailants had taken jewellery and valuable objects from a sideboard in her bedroom.

'Unluckily for them, we made our entrance at the precise moment when our honourable friends were brewing portions of cocaine for purposes of trade.'

'Bloody hell!' I said.

The girl did a somersault, yelling out a shriek of triumph as she turned head over heels. The sergeant removed her dark spectacles. 'Luckily for you, Signorina, these bruises on your eyes testify to the fact that you were forcibly compelled to stay with Brizzi. Then there's the proof of these photographs.' So saying, he showed the girl a sequence of images taken at the villa when the gangsters were holding her naked and dragging her away.

'Who took these?' she asked in bewilderment.

'My men had been stationed for a couple of hours in the garden. They had heard the rumour that the gang would turn up at the Polish woman's villa to settle accounts.'

'So why didn't you intervene to set me free and get my boyfriend out of the clutches of those villains? You just stood there and watched while they beat him to within an inch of his life.'

'No, no,' said the sergeant. 'We weren't just watching. We managed to take quite a lot of photographs through the window of you being beaten up, and if we'd have arrested them that night, we'd have missed the chance to catch them with the cocaine! Think about it: for assault they'd have got a maximum of a couple of years, but for drugs they're looking at a minimum of another ten. OK, we let them knock you about a bit, but now you can breathe freely for a good twelve years. You are as free to enjoy your lives together as chaffinches in spring.'

'Thanks, sergeant, but seeing as you've gone this far, you don't think you could put his mother, the Pole, inside as well?'

The sergeant gave a raucous laugh. 'You're not just a pretty face. You're sharp-eyed and smart as well. But heed my advice. Keep well away from drugs if you want to live a long and happy life.'

# CHAPTER 17

## The Bindula Boys

*B*indula is a dialect variation of the verb *abbindolare*, which means 'to make fun of someone'. The *Bindula* boys were a group of idle smart asses, unsurpassable champions of the practical joke, totally ingenious in the diabolical capers they could think up and pull off.

They used to devise all manner of trickery at the expense of any poor simpleton in the valley or beyond. They had no regard for anyone, no pity for man or beast, but their favourite victim was an ex-soldier with the *Arditi*, known as 'Pacioch', a candid, credulous nincompoop. He looked like a tree trunk from which daisies might sprout: the classic, good-natured booby; the ideal scapegoat, in other words, for those good-for-nothing charlatans.

One of the leaders of the gang rejoiced in the name of Gratacu (Itchy-arse), the local word for a nettle. One day he was visiting a friend who ran a junkyard for cars above the town. In the workshop, they were dismantling an old car, a facsimile of the famed Bugatti, with the intention of using only some pieces and scrapping the rest. They had already removed the sides, including the doors, pulled out the dash board, hauled away the lid of the boot and stripped the engine down to a few bolts. The sight of the remains of that car gave Gratacu an outrageous idea: he asked his friend to lend him that wreck, just as it was, for half a day. Then, with the help of two fellow *Bindula*, he busied himself reassembling once more the glorious automobile. They put the engine to one side, then, like the master craftsmen-tricksters they were, the three of them made use of a roll of fishing tackle to secure each part to a rope under the chassis: they then let out the various lines, pulling them together and tying them up behind the boot. In other words, they had just stitched together the entire chassis.

Now that the trap was laid, they set off pushing the car, which was now held together by pieces of string, down the hill to the harbour, in front of the chalet housing the Mira-Lago bar. When they were in sight of the chalet, the two *Bindula* boys squatted down behind the boot and made it roll into the piazza. Gratacu was inside the car, pretending to drive.

When they reached the bar, all the customers got up in amazement to have a look at a vehicle which was a museum piece. The supposed driver got out and called over to Pacioch, who was quietly sitting outside, like a somewhat dim-witted cat.

'Would you do me a favour, if it's not too much trouble . . .'

Pacioch jumped to his feet at once. To be of service to one of the *Bindula* boys was for him an honour beyond compare.

'There's no water in the radiator, and the whole thing nearly seized up. Would you be good enough to go into the bar and ask for a bucket of water?'

The poor booby rushed off in a state of excitement. It was rare for them to show so much faith in him! He came dashing back with the pail of water and found the bonnet already up. Gratacu seized hold of the bucket: 'Thanks, I'll see to it, but if you could close the door for me. I've gone and left it open, and for goodness sake, it's a very valuable, delicate car, so go easy, eh?'

Pacioch did his best to proceed as gently as possible, but as he pushed the door, it slammed shut with a loud bang. Behind the boot, the two accomplices pulled the trip wire: they tugged the lines fixed to the various bits of the car so that the whole structure crashed noisily to the ground. The doors collapsed, the dashboard was hurled into the air, the bonnet flew off and ended up on top of Gratacu. The swine let out a despairing groan and flopped to the ground as though dead. Like two jacks-in-the-box, the other pair suddenly appeared from behind the now-ruined car, making a great display of terror and horror: 'Christ in heaven, Pacioch, what have you done?' asked one.

'Did you toss in a bomb?' demanded the second.

Poor Pacioch was devastated. The customers outside the bar joined in. 'Oh, what a disaster!' was the cry.

'I don't know,' stammered Pacioch, 'I only closed the door . . . very gently.'

Some went over to help Gratacu, who was still playing the part of a recently expired corpse. When he came round, Gratacu went into a rage and attacked Pacioch like a bolt from a catapult. 'You bloody fool, don't you realise you have just wrecked a jewel fit for any collection? We had only borrowed it for an hour. Now who's going to pay for it?'

One of the tricksters screamed, pointing at the inside of the bonnet: 'Look, the engine's gone! It's disappeared!'

Everybody started poking around. A boy pointed his finger at the huge plane tree. 'It's up there in the tree! It's got caught up between two branches.'

It is unnecessary to state that the organisers of the whole trick had put it there before the event.

'Would someone like to tell me,' interjected one of the group of friends, 'what on earth kind of blow this creature must have delivered to shoot an engine up as high as that? He's a force of nature. He has the muscles of a wild beast. We should only let him walk about with two circles of iron around his arms to restrain the propulsive strength of his biceps. Otherwise he'd be a public menace.'

Poor Pacioch looked about like a lost soul, swallowed hard in mortification . . . then quickly made up his mind.

'All right, tell me where to go to get these two irons attached.'

'To the blacksmith's,' came the chorus of reply. And so they all accompanied him in procession to the blacksmith's to see him fixed up with real irons, which, as luck would have it, were all ready . . . and just the right size!

## CHAPTER 18

### Wedding in the Coptic Rite

A month went by and Stumpy was released from hospital. His mother, under the pretext that he needed time to recuperate, took him to Ascona in the Canton of Ticino, where the father's side of the family had a house. He did not stay there as much as three days before making his way back to Porto Valtravaglia. He arrived on his motorboat, the one which had caused him to lose his hand. She, as beautiful as any pharaoh's wife, had been there on the quay for God knows how long waiting for him. The boat moored, he jumped out, put his arms round her and led her off on a wild dance: round and round they went, and the upshot was that both of them ended up in the lake. All the folk on the fore-shore rushed over, but the two re-emerged laughing, waving their arms and spraying water over all those who had come to help.

However, Stumpy's mother would not hear of her son getting together with 'that Egyptian whore'. Right reason or none, she was out to dissuade him. To begin with, she sold the villa to German tourists so as to force her son and his girlfriend to move out. Stumpy had always depended on his mother for cash, so how was he to make ends meet now? All that was left to him was his motorboat, and he offered his services to a company which transported goods and passengers. Nofret found a job as a waitress in the restaurant-hotel down by the harbour, and together they rented a cottage nearby. I often met up with them, and they were very happy. They wanted to organise a grand wedding, but they were in no position to do so. Stumpy was still married to a woman from Lugano, even if they had been separated for more than five years. Divorce was legal in Switzerland, but he was an Italian citizen, so it would have been invalid in Italy.

One Sunday they invited all their friends, who were legion, to the square facing the harbour. We children were also asked along. They had decided to celebrate a fake wedding, with a ceremony in the Coptic rite. A Greek glass-blower and his entire community turned up, including an austere man dressed in a red tunic and tube-like hat with a circular form at the top. The Greek group, women included, were in folk dress and had brought various instruments with them – trumpets, violas and accordions. They started singing in tones which had a certain resemblance to Gregorian chant.

The bride was wearing a very high-necked, subtly plissé dress, which came down to her feet like a colonnade. He had on a dark suit which was not unlike an evening suit.

Emotion ran high throughout the whole ceremony, during which everybody held candles and rang bells. A few women could not hold back their tears.

They had laid out a big table on the square by the lakeside, and served a gargantuan meal offered by the fishermen. In the midst of the celebrations, even the parish priest came along to embrace the newly-weds, even though they had been united by his rivals. I have always thought that priest was a man of unusual spirit! The brass band struck up a waltz, and the piazza was transformed into a gigantic ballroom.

At sunset, the whole gathering accompanied the bride and groom down to the quay where the motorboat, now adorned with flowers, awaited them. Nofret and her Rizzul jumped in at the same time, and, with a great waving of hands, off went the boat. The band struck up a quick-tempo *paso doble*. 'A pity the Polish woman could not have been here,' someone remarked. 'I bet she'd have been in tears as well!'

We were moving away from the harbour when we heard a loud bang, and turned to look out over the lake. The motorboat reared up, seemed to take off, then plunged prow-first into the water and sank. It vanished from view. The fishermen rushed to their boats, another motorboat was put out and in a few minutes they were at the spot where the disaster had occurred. A boy dived in from the rescue vessel . . . the fishermen came on the scene, and some of them, too, went into the water. They pulled them out, put them on the boats, the doctor arrived . . . one of the Greeks had gone to fetch him. The boats moored. Nofret and her beloved were laid out on the grass, one beside the other. The doctor had a strange implement with him, a kind of suction pump with which he sucked out all the water the two young folk had ingested, but it was all to no avail.

We all stood around petrified. The parish priest knelt down, gave a blessing and said a prayer. The two corpses could not be moved until the on-duty magistrate in Luino arrived. We all stood around in silence. People arrived from nearby villages, and a large circle formed. One of those who had just come on the scene began to whisper some form of comment, but he was asked to be silent.

The sun was setting. The shadows on the square lengthened into interminable shapes. Some sobs were heard, and there were many who could not hold back tears.

# CHAPTER 19

## At Grandfather's

At the age of fourteen, I was admitted to the Brera Academy after a very exacting selection process. Out of the one hundred and fifty applicants, only forty passed the examinations.

During the Easter holidays I went to stay with my grandparents in Lomellina. On arrival, I was astonished not to be met by the usual swarms of midges and mosquitoes. No wonder! It was only March and the onset of those hellish insects was still some time off. On the other hand, at nightfall, the croaking of the frogs rose up, only to end quite suddenly with a succession of splashes as they plunged into the canals and waterways. It was not for nothing that we were in Sartirana, a name which means 'Leaping Frog'.

I could scarcely recognise my grandfather's farmhouse when I got there. The climbing plants clinging to the columns of the arches under the quadrilateral portico were in bloom. There were dashes of colour on the walls of the stables and wood-store as well, and all that's before we got to the orchard! As soon as I went with Granddad Bristìn on donkey back onto the bridge over the canal, the orchards appeared before us, laid out like an enormous chessboard of an infinite number of mosaic tesserae in an impossible perspective. The larger and smaller pawns were the fruit trees which had produced blossoms galore. My grandfather savoured my amazement in silence, then whispered to me: 'Don't just look with your eyes, look with your nose too.'

'Look with my nose?'

'Yes, smell, listen to the scents and perfumes.'

'Ah yes, I hear them. They're very good.'

'Always be aware that you must know how to read smells and scents. For example, come over here, under this cherry tree. Sniff gently, breathing softly. Listen, it has an almost salty after-taste . . . this one over here is also a cherry tree, but it has a sweeter scent, it's almost rounded and is more intense than the other one. And do you know why? Because the first tree shed its blossoms too early, and so got a chill. The other wasn't in such a hurry to bloom and so avoided the problem!'

'And you can understand that from the scent?'

'Certainly, and from the scent I already know what the fruit will be like: the one that the frost got to will have its fruit late and thin, but the second ones will be plump, full and beauti-fully scented. It's the same with people. If a baby gets a serious illness, it needs time, care, food and warmth before it recovers, and you can tell from its smell when it's not at its best.'

'So why do doctors never smell you when they come to see you?'

'Because they've forgotten ancient medicine. In the Salerno treatises that taught doctors how to go about examining a patient, it is written: "Feel the skin and muscles from head to toe, listen to how the blood is circulating, test the skin with the fingers to discover where it is sweet, damp or where it is dry and above all smell, guess the humour, the salted, the bitter, where it is pleasing and where it emanates odours . . . which is a way of saying where it stinks."'

'Really! How much you know, Granddad! Did you ever study medicine?'

'No, but I'm a curious old soul that's never easily satisfied with the notions books and academics try to palm you off with. Look, it doesn't matter whether you are talking about trees, potatoes, flowers or tomatoes: if an apple is bitten by an insect or infected by a virus, it immediately reacts by changing smell, even before its appearance changes. It's a sign it gives you gratis. It's the same with a man or a woman. His or her pleasing smell doesn't just inform you that they are in good health, it also tells you something about their mood. If they give off a whiff of perfume, it means they are experiencing some emotion, that perhaps they like you and you can be happy with that, and if then you feel a thrill or your heart starts beating faster, you can be sure that in the same way you'll be sprinkling your own message of contented scents in the air!'

'And everyone will be aware of it? All you have to do is sniff around?'

'Unfortunately not. If a man falls in love and looks into his girlfriend's eyes, he might notice that she's pale or that she's flushed, that her palms are damp with perspiration because of the emotion, but he won't listen to her smell, he won't hear it because we have lost the sense of smell. We have been castrated of this basic sense.'

I was astonished. 'What a shame! And it's too late to do anything about it?'

'Well, you know . . . by practising with method and, above all, with constancy, maybe a remedy can be found.'

'Sniffing exercises?'

'Exactly. Training to use your nostrils on everything and every person, as the animals do. A dog that meets you sniffs at you. If he doesn't like your smell, he goes off in disgust and you can count yourself lucky if he does not pee on you as well.'

'Granddad, you're making a fool of me! So you're telling me that to get my sense of smell back, I've got to become a dog! I've got to go on all fours, sniff the legs and maybe even the backside of people I meet!'

Grandfather laughed heartily. 'Congratulations! A great parry. In any case, I advise you to try it, without going over the top. You'll acquire a splendid culture that way.'

'A culture on stinks?'

'Yes. Did you never wonder why women, and nowadays some men too, dose themselves more and more in perfume?'

'To cover body odours and rancid sweat.'

'Don't exaggerate. It's true that spraying yourself every so often with a delicate perfume can produce a pleasing effect: it is excess that does the harm. It's a concealment born of distrust of the products of our own excellent glands. Professor Trangipane told me that as early as the eighteenth century, bewigged noblemen discovered they emitted odours according to their states of mind, and that these signals were clearly decipherable and legible by the nose. So, to prevent other people from using their smell to find out character, personality, emotions and hypocrisy, which has an especially stomach-churning smell, they preferred to cancel all smell with doses of perfume.'

'Granddad, are you telling me that if I exercise properly . . . all I need is one good sniff, and no one will be able to put one over me?'

'Absolutely right! Everything in nature has a language: people's way of gesturing, gesticulating, their way of walking, of sitting down, of shaking hands . . . their way of using their voice and articulating words . . . everything is an encyclopedia of invaluable signs. It's as though you were to pull people's clothes off and see them naked, as they really are, with their buttocks and prattle exposed to the winds.'

At the end of this mad tirade from Grandfather, I wanted to clap wildly: 'Where do you get these ideas from? And don't tell me they come to you by chance, or that they're just born all by themselves, like the radishes in the orchard.'

'No, nothing comes from nothing, and it doesn't matter whether you are talking about some idea spat out of a man's brain or a fart shot out of a monkey's arse. Not even a sneeze explodes on its own, by itself. Every intuition is always born by crossing different notions, often opposing ones, just as you do when you are grafting plants together.'

'You started off talking about sniffing, now you're on to grafts and farts, so where are you going to end up?'

'At knowledge, at finding out about things, searching, checking. Never be content with facile rules, or with the lying books they give you to read at school.'

'That's enough, Granddad. You're making my head spin with all these metaphors. All right, I'll bear them in mind. But you were a peasant, so how did you manage to teach yourself so much . . . I mean, to graft together all these bits of knowledge?'

'I'll tell you: the ace in my pack was Don Gaetano. This holy man went straight to the seminary from Turin Polytechnic, where he was about to graduate. He was no run-of-the-mill spirit; he argued about everything, even about dogmas. A couple of centuries ago they would have burned him at the stake, at the very least. So as soon as he took his vows, they packed him off as a kind of punishment to a parish in the Monferrato countryside. I don't know if it was out of a sense of vocation or out of a desire to overcome boredom, but Don Gaetano decided to open a school for the children of the district. He had a competition. I was seven, and I presented myself together with a dozen other hopefuls like me. That teacher was a real performer. He managed to make us passionate about any subject, he was able to transform everything into a laughter-filled game, or into stories more captivating than any fable. Just imagine, I was so taken by the desire to learn that I used to run away from the fields so as not to miss a single one of his lessons. Look, I am no Pico della Mirandola when it comes to memory, but if they tell me a story or if I read about a problem or a fact which catches my imagination, I can recount it to you a month later, without getting one word wrong!'

'Don Gaetano's ideas were slightly different from those of the bosses, that is from the landowners and mill-owners. He would often launch terrifying broadsides at them, even during his sermons, until one day someone laid a trap for him. He lived in a house attached to the church wall, so to get to the church all he had to do was climb a flight of stairs to the sacristy. One morning, he was coming down after mass but someone had had the bright idea of sawing off the first two steps. He fell down like a sack of potatoes. He broke his leg and femur, and was laid up in bed for I don't know how long. Every day, as soon as I got home from the fields, I used to go and keep him company. As a way of thanking me, he used to read a couple of chapters to me, and when he got tired I read to him. I can't tell you how much we read together: history, philosophy and even books of rational mechanics. And then novels, and we even read texts that were forbidden by the Vatican, for example, the edition of one of the gospels translated in the sixteenth century from the Greek to Mantuan dialect, and published secretly in Geneva. The translator was put on trial for heresy and burned alive.'

'So explain this to me: why did you not become a priest yourself?'

'Excuse me, did it never cross your mind that if your grandfather had become a priest, your mother would never have been born and you wouldn't be here listening to me?'

'Ah! It was all to make sure that I was born! Thank you very much. Anyway, Granddad, to listen to all your subversive speeches, nobody would ever know that you were educated by a parish priest!'

'Never judge anyone by the clothes he wears, my boy! In any case, I do not owe the whole of my education to him. Do you remember Professor Trangipane, the one who used to teach in the Faculty of Agrarian Studies in the University of Alessandria, and who came here once with his students? He and his lads used to come and see me here before you were born. They would turn up, determined not to stand any nonsense, and fire loads of questions on Applied Agronomy at me. For the sake of my *bella figura*, I had to master theory: I got my head down over the texts the professor got for me, as though I were doing exams.'

'It's a pity you didn't, Granddad. You would certainly have got a degree.'

'Yes, that's just what the professor said . . . but he always added that it would have been a crime. "Dear Bristìn, today you are a phenomenon. You are the only teaching peasant in the world. With a degree, you'd only be an ordinary professor!"'

# CHAPTER 20

## The Voyage of the Argonauts

When I celebrated my sixteenth birthday, I had already been attending the Brera for some years. I got up every morning at half past five, went racing along the lakeside without drawing breath and, keeping an ear cocked for the train from Luino as it appeared and disappeared in and out of the tunnels, I took part in a daily competition to see which of us would reach the station first. I lost the race only once, because of a mêlée at the finishing line: it was pitch black and I did not notice a gas pipe placed across the road.

I often jumped onto the train when it was already moving: my travelling companions would cheer lustily, and if I managed to get a foot on the running board, they would grab hold of me and pull me into the carriage.

The train normally had five or six coaches. The second-class one was divided into eight-person compartments, while the rest of the compartments were third class, that is, they consisted of the one open space. The young people preferred this one since it allowed us to mix together in a squash of males and females, students, young office-workers and a few factory-hands. They all got on in small groups at various stations until the whole train was crowded.

With a few friends from the Valtravaglia, I took upon myself the role of story-teller, and there were others who sang to the

151

accompaniment of guitars or accordions. At Caldè, a complete brass band would often get on: the two who played the flute and the slide-trombone were studying at the *Conservatorio*. The upshot was that our coach rejoiced in the nickname of the *caravan de ciuch*, the drunkards' caravan.

Every so often I would desert that pandemonium and take refuge in another carriage to get on with some study, but I was not always successful. My companions would come looking for me, and often prevailed on me to tell them at least a couple of tales. At that time, my repertoire was somewhat limited, so to avoid repeating myself, I was obliged to invent more and more new adventures. I cast in a grotesque, ironical light famous historical enterprises, like the story of *Garibaldi and the Thousand*, when the boat remained moored at Quarto because three members of the expedition were missing. If we do not reach the full complement, we can't depart, was the nervous comment of General Giuseppe Garibaldi, because we can't really call it *The Expedition of the Nine Hundred and Ninety-Seven*. They decide to seize the first people who come along: two drunks, one called Nino Bixio and the other Santorre di Santarosa, and finally a man who had just escaped from the prison in Genoa.

It was in the same random way that there, in the third-class coach, other impossible tales, all pulled inside out, concerning Christopher Columbus, Ulysses and other epic heroes were conceived.

The *Odyssey*, in particular, became for me an inexhaustible storehouse of satirical, comic motifs. There was the dilemma of Ulysses, desperate to put to sea and get back home, and Poseidon on the look-out for him, peeping out from underwater in the belly of a whale. Poor aquatic pachyderm, forced to live open-mouthed, continually rocked by vomiting fits!

Right on cue, a storm rises and Ulysses is tossed onto another shore. There he is in the land of the Phaeacians, then in the arms of Nausicaa. When he gets on his way again, Poseidon pounds the calm sea with his hands, causing the waves to rise higher than the peak of Musadino. The ship breaks apart and this time the hero is thrown ashore on Aeaea, this time into the arms of Circe. He allows himself to be overwhelmed by passion and to get up to all manner of escapades with the greedy enchantress. His companions, meantime, transformed into filthy pigs, are bored and find their only enjoyment in watching Ulysses make a fool of himself with all his tawdry cavortings with that sow of a witch, Circe.

But it's clear that Ulysses had never had the slightest intention of returning home. He was more than happy with his round of non-stop affairs. The idea of going back to stony Ithaca, to a wife who spent every moment of her time weaving cloth, and to a flee-ridden dog that was always between his feet did not attract him one little bit.

The truth of it was that it was he who went in search of storms to hold him back, so much so that before setting off from a coast, he would go out of his way to make sure that the god of the sea was wide awake and in a bad temper with him. Indeed, when he realises that Poseidon is getting fed up with persecuting him, what does he do? He deliberately lands on the island of the Cyclops and upsets Polyphemus, who just happens to be Poseidon's son, gets him drunk and sticks a flaming stake into his one eye. What a swine he was, this Ulysses! You could have wagered that the boy's father, god of the depths, was bound to unleash every giant wave he could. But whichever way you look at it, is it conceivable that a skilled master seaman like Ulysses would have taken ten years to get away from the coasts of Sicily?

Ah yes, because, look at it this way, that was the island he was always manoeuvring around. He sailed close to every cliff, went up every inlet thereabouts and perhaps touched Tunisia, but only briefly.

When he returned to Ithaca it was only by accident. He was convinced he was on Zacynthus! 'Damnation, here I am back home!' To avoid being recognised, he dressed up as a tramp, but the mongrel went and recognised him, so he gave him a such a kick that he killed him. 'Papa, Papa!' exclaimed Telemachus, all sure of himself. Only Ulysses could dispatch a dog with one kick like that. 'Yes, it's me, but not a word to your mother!'

'Why?'

'I don't trust her, she's got those suitors pressing her to get her into bed with them.'

'But Papa, she hasn't done it with any of them.'

'Well, you never can tell. Can you swear on the Bible?'

'Please, Papa, don't bring politics into it.'

No sooner said than done. Ulysses bends his bow and skewers all those bastards of suitors. Only then does his wife recognise him. 'Welcome home, my husband.' Hugs and kisses. Groans and languid sighs.

In no time it's dawn.

'Very sorry, but I've got to go!'

'Already? Did you only come for a change of underwear?'

'I'm coming too, father.'

'OK, but get a move on, because the ship is ready and waiting, and the wind is in the right direction. Bye, bye, my wife. Don't worry, I'll be back soon. In about twenty years.'

End of story.

As is obvious, I am only giving an outline of those stories I performed on the train journey to Milan. Every time I did them, I put in fresh twists, or improvised new vocal or mime acts. Often I was obliged to climb up on the bench in the centre of the carriage so that everyone could follow me. In short, the carriage of the Luino-Gallarate-Milan (Porta Garibaldi station) express was for years my stage, with stalls invariably sold-out and appreciative!

The spectators were not only young men and women, but also often included more mature, less regular travellers. Some, after a while, went away annoyed or displeased over certain lines they considered inappropriate, but for the most part the casual listeners who came along were unexpectedly enthusiastic. Among them was one singular, middle-aged gentleman who at times exploded in raucous, infectious laughter. The gentleman was Professor Civolla, historian and anthropologist of the University of Milan, to whom I referred earlier. One evening, returning home on my own later than usual, I found him alone in a compartment. He invited me to sit beside him and started firing questions at me. He knew I was studying at the Brera, and that I had had the finest *fabulatori* of the Valtravaglia as masters (apart from anything else, he himself lived in Porto), but he wondered what sources I had been drawing on for some of the grotesque motifs I had adopted to turn the original form of the situations I narrated upside down.

'Well,' I replied, 'I have only applied the parodying techniques I learned from the story-tellers in Porto when they wanted to trip people up.'

'No, no,' he insisted, 'I know these techniques too, I've grown up with them. I'm talking about the underlying paradoxes.'

I looked at him in some embarrassment, then admitted I had not understood the question. 'Excuse me, professor, what do you mean by underlying paradoxes?'

'They are the ones taken from ancient historical tradition . . . do you know Lucian of Samosata?'

'No, who is he?'

'An extraordinary poet from the second century, Greek obviously, the satirical author who brought the technique of paradox to its highest perfection. He would take an almost sacred story and toss it around a bit. Achilles, you're telling me he was a generous-hearted hero? Anything but; he was a hysterical, egocentric, mad criminal! A right bastard who was engaged to Iphigenia, the gentle daughter of Agamemnon, and then when the oracle at Delphi intoned: "Achaeans, if you want to conquer Troy you must slaughter like a goat the virgin beloved of Achilles", what does Achilles, son of Peleus, do? He takes Iphigenia by the arm and, as though it doesn't matter a jot to him, escorts her to the sacred tree under which she is to be sacrificed!'

And he went on to tell me about Ulysses betraying his friend Philoctetes who had been bitten in the thigh by a poisonous snake. Poor Philoctetes with his injured leg turning gangrenous was convinced by the honest Ulysses to disembark at Lemnos, a desert island. He then abandons him like a marooned sailor, leaving him to his own devices and telling him to get with it! But, not long afterwards, Ulysses is informed by the oracle that without the infallible bow in the possession of that gangrenous, abandoned soul, the Achaeans will never manage to get the better of the Trojans. Countermand: back to square one. Ulysses returns to the island, dressed as a travelling merchant, tricks Philoctetes into giving up the bow and goes on his way.

In this way, one after the other, the professor drew me portraits of a series of heroes, queens, gods and goddesses whom at school they had given us as role-models, but who, once the commonplaces of rhetoric had been turned on their head, were made to appear, some more than others, like a band of swindlers, hypocrites and opportunists.

I was literally fascinated by Civolla's conversation. We reached our destination in no time but we were so engrossed by what we were saying, I in asking questions and he in recounting, that we almost missed our stop. As we said good night to each other, we promised to meet again a few days later. It was a Tuesday and promptly on Thursday I presented myself at his home in the Antico Cambio Palace. The professor lived in the attic flat, immediately under the roof, in a large single room which covered the entire area of the palace. There were tables piled high with papers and books, a book case which covered a whole wall, and four glass doors inset in arches which opened onto a big balcony. Without more ado, he let me see one of his most recent discoveries, the reproduction of a kind of map from the fifth century AD which showed the mythical voyage of the Argonauts. I felt myself drowning in a well of ignorance. Who were these Argonauts? What had they got up to, where were they from, where were they going?

The greatest talent of a teacher, according to Pliny the Elder, was never to let his own knowledge overburden the pupil's less well-stocked brain, and this was beyond all question one of Professor Civolla's gifts. As he showed me the map, he called my attention to how it was designed without regard for the actual alignment of the coasts and rivers. Everything was highly approximate. 'Look, the position of Corinth is marked here, which is where the Argonauts are supposed to have set off from some four thousand odd years ago. And here is Pagasae, the port and shipyard where, according to the myth, the ship *Argo*, which gives us the name Argonaut, was constructed. The bards of this epic predated the tales of the *Iliad* and the *Odyssey* by some considerable time. On the expedition, as you will certainly know, there was Jason in the role of captain, and, just to jolly things along, Hercules, who after one or two labours was taking a short vacation, the two Dioscuri, Theseus and a great number of other heroes employed to provide a bit of ballast. There was also Orpheus, the great musician and well-known enchanter of the Sirens.

'The expedition was, as usual, arranged for purposes of robbery and piracy. The idea was to reach Colchis on the Black Sea, where, under the protection of a dragon, the Golden Fleece was to be found. The Golden Fleece was the woollen coat of a ram which was itself golden, and was endowed with extraordinary powers. Here's an interesting detail: the ship had been constructed with timber gifted by Athena, so at the launch the heroes noticed that the vessel could speak. A deep voice emanated from the head of an ox on the prow giving indications of the route to be followed or of impending storms and, when the ship was becalmed, it had a repertoire of beguiling tales.

'The expedition set off towards the Dardanelles, through the Strait of Bosphorus and at last arrived at the Black Sea, obviously after having overcome many problems en route: hostile populations, cliffs and, jutting out of the sea, rocks which could be pushed close together by the winds.

'When they landed at Colchis, the king ordered Jason to undertake a series of very severe tests, like yoking to the plough two savage, fire-breathing oxen which lashed out ferociously with their brazen hooves. Luckily for Jason, the king's young daughter, Medea, herself endowed with great intelligence and magic powers, fell in love with him and, even if it meant betraying her father, did all she could to help him in all his trials, including the one requiring him to destroy an army of warriors born from sowing the teeth of a dragon, no less, in the ground. And all this without as much as a coffee break.

'Second episode: Medea, with the collaboration of Orpheus, puts the dragon to sleep long enough to allow the Argonauts to snatch the Golden Fleece without too much trouble. Medea, now deeply in love with Jason, decides to follow him. The hero promises her that the moment they reach a peaceful, safe place, he will take her as his bride. The king, the father of the young enchantress, goes absolutely wild at the news. Those bastards from Achaea have pilfered his fleece, and now they're off with the daughter whom he had promised to a neighbouring king. In a rage, he gives chase to the thieves' ship.

'So as to foil her father who, with his ships packed with warriors, was catching up on the Argonauts, Medea executes an act of unthinkable ferocity: she slaughters her younger brother whom she had brought along with her. She tears him to pieces and scatters his severed limbs in the fields along the coast. In despair, the king moors at the shore and stops to search, with the help of his men, for the fragments of his son's body. This horrendous stratagem gives the Achaeans the advantage and allows them to reach the Straits of the Bosphorus, but alas! the opening is blocked by another of the king's fleets which had gone ahead. Once again they are saved by Medea who shows Jason a different escape route, up the mouth of the Danube which opens right in front of them.'

As he spoke, the professor showed me on the Byzantine map the fugitives' only possible route. 'Hercules did not agree: "If we go this way, we will have to proceed to the land of the Germans, then across a great chain of mountains with the ship on our backs." "You've got to choose: either extend the journey or accelerate death!" replies Medea. "The girl's right," comments the ox's skull on the prow, "take it or leave it." '

'After a few months, raiding and slaughtering here and there to ensure their own survival, they reach the sources of the Danube. With the ship on their backs and labouring like beasts, they come out on the Rhine, and from there, sailing for several moons against the current, they enter Lake Constance. More moons. They curse their way across the Alps, still with their vessel on their backs. They finally reach Italy and come down into Lake Maggiore.'

I stood there with my mouth hanging open. My eyes, too, were wide open.

'Incredible! The Argonauts arriving here in our land! OK, it's a myth, but we're not going to find it's merely nonsense, are we?'

'Certainly, you can expect anything with myths, but this adventure was recounted by at least three separate bards, several centuries apart from one another, and they were all in agreement on the route of the voyage. Look here, I've got another two maps. Compare them with the first. The red line which marks the journey goes in the same direction on all three. Look, this mark shows the spot where the ship berths.'

'But it's on our shores! This must be the mouth of the Tresa and here, this inlet . . .'

'You're right. It is our coastline. The temple of the oracle used to be in the port of the Valtravaglia.'

'We used to have an oracle here?'

'And what's so odd about that? Every ancient civilisation had at least a couple. In our lands, in these valleys, we had the Celts, or more exactly the Senones, in other words the primordial Celtic race.'

'All right, so what did these Argonauts have to do with this oracle?'

'They had to perform a sacrificial rite inside the temple which was hewn out at the foot of the waterfall, in order to purge themselves of all the crimes and pillage carried out in Colchis and on the rest of the voyage. Medea, in particular, had to purify herself, free herself of the ignominy of having killed her brother and dispersed his limbs. She knew that the commission of that crime would cause her dreadful labour pains. Every one of the Argonauts had to be present at that birth: Medea's pain would liberate their consciences too. As is always the case, it is the woman who does the purgation for everyone.'

'The daughter of the king of Colchis is laid out on the temple floor, and then her sufferings begin. Medea is seized by terrible contractions. Spasms follow hard one after the other, causing her face to be deformed by pain. The unborn child screams from inside his mother's womb. At first, they are meaningless screeches, but gradually they are transformed into a series of curses of unthinkable ferocity: it is the voice of the oracle speaking through the cries of the child. The Argonauts listen to the list of all their misdeeds . . . the body of Medea has become almost transparent and inside her womb the child thrashes about and continues to scream insults and threats. The heroes bend down until their faces are level with the floor: soaked with sweat, they weep. The labour is interminable . . . at last the son of Jason and Medea is born, the very child whom, not long afterwards, his mother will slaughter to take her revenge!'

At the conclusion of the story, I too felt damp with sweat and it was with difficulty that I asked: 'Is it from that awful birth that our valley takes its name?'

'Indeed,' concluded the professor. '*Valle del Travaglio*, the Valley of Labour, nowadays Valtravaglia. After Medea's labour pains.'

'Incredible. I thought it referred to the labours of work.'

'Perhaps that is the correct origin. In fact it is as well never to place undue trust in etymologies which are overloaded with mystic tragedy!'

'In any case, whether it's a question of a reliable event or of some fantasy, the whole epic is a wonderful tale. It's strange that Homer didn't grab it for himself.'

'In that case, you take full advantage and reinvent it at once! Hurry up because the ancients always return, and they claim everything back, including your newest fantasies!'

# CHAPTER 21

## *Physical Harmony*

For us children who lived along the lakeside, what game could rival splashing about in the water, diving from rocks and rowing on any kind of craft? We did not view any of these activities as sports or organised disciplines but as enjoyable pastimes in which we challenged each other to see who was fastest, most agile or most daring. Our life was one long wallow in water.

On the beach, we took note of how the older boys swam, especially if they showed signs of possessing experience and style. Often we took our courage in both hands and asked them for a few hints, in other words, asked them to be to some extent our masters.

Thus I learned that in swimming the most important thing is not strength but harmony: everything, every part of the body, every limb must glide smoothly, without upsetting the delicate balance between movement and breathing. Working in the theatre a dozen or so years later, I discovered that producing the maximum impact with the minimum of effort and gesture was the principal rule for every mime and every actor worth his salt. It was not a particularly stunning discovery. Shakespeare himself, through the words of Hamlet, advised actors to move and perform with intensity and 'temperance', rather than with any useless waste of energy.

But let us go back to swimming. I felt in my element in the water, even if, as happens with all boys who are passionate about a game but lack discipline and measure, I tended to go over the score. Often, even when the sun was shining, my companions and I came out of the lake blue and trembling with the cold. There was the danger of getting caught by icy currents which could easily cause painful cramps, and which could have dire consequences. Since we always went swimming in groups, we were in a position to help one another. If one of us was seized by spasms of *crampul*, we knew how to massage the muscle affected back to life.

Our second great passion was rowing. The dream of each of us was one day to acquire a boat of his own, but our limited resources made this dream almost unachievable. Occasionally, we were able to take advantage of the generosity of some holiday-maker who allowed us to play about in their boat, and more frequently we were able to go out on the boats of the fishermen, but to sit behind an oar was for us a driving need: breathe in, arch, take the strain, rise, breathe out, stretch, release, bend, and back to the beginning, all the while dipping oars in water. I had discovered that, as with swimming, perfect coordination of movement ensures maximum speed with minimum effort. The key to progress, however, was the ability to train constantly, but with no boat of my own, how was this to be done? The solution to the problem lay in Milan.

Every year in Milan, those who studied at the Brera were taken on to set up exhibitions at the *Fiera Campionaria*, the Trade Fair. The pay was reasonably good, but the work was murderous. It involved developing projects, completing decorations by painting or erecting models, putting up various plastic books, scribbling out gigantic letters or improvising at the last minute solutions to publicity difficulties.

I was not yet seventeen when I was employed to prepare an enormous stand which should have taken at least a month. At the inauguration of the fair, I was totally exhausted. I had spent the previous two nights without a wink of sleep, and when I got home it was already daybreak. Before leaving the fair, I crossed the entire pavilion where the prototypes of canoes and competition-class rowing boats with a mobile rowing mechanism were on display. There was one which had fascinated me, a 'one-off' with ash-wood hull and sliding-seat.

When I got to my bed, I slept uninterruptedly for twenty hours. Just before waking up, I dreamt of that racing skiff skimming lightly over the water, and it was me who, with a casual touch of the oars, made it go. After a while, the boat took off into the air and I was in flight. I passed over the wharf, flew over the great harbour, touched the top of the church tower and glided through the clouds back down to the lake . . .

At the end of the week, I was back at the *Fiera* to draw my wages for the installation work, a decent sum of money. I went into the pavilion where my boat was on display and asked if I could have a closer look at it, to examine it properly. The attendant stared at me with ill-disguised, annoyed condescension and said: 'But please, don't touch!'

I looked back at him with a malicious smile and then asked: 'Can I at least give it a little lick?' The attendant gazed at me in surprise and then burst out laughing, but from that moment he relaxed. He helped me to lift it, weigh it and contemplate its design from all angles, both right way up and upside down. It was a masterpiece, as beautiful and elegant as a dolphin . . .

no, even more beautiful: it was a mermaid fit to win any competition!

I bought it. I put nearly all my capital into it, but it was by any standards worth every penny. To keep a close eye on the carrier who would be transporting it to the lake, I oversaw in person the packaging and loading, and then, so as not to let it out of my sight, I climbed into the cabin beside the lorry driver.

For the launch, I was down at the quay at seven o'clock in the morning. Almost all my friends in the gang came along to give a hand in lowering the skiff into the water. Each one had his own enthusiastic comments to make.

As we raised the hull, my legs were shaking as though I were about to make love to it. The balance was so precarious that at every movement I risked keeling over, and I immediately shipped water, but as soon as I gripped the oars in my hands and began to move backwards and forwards on the sliding-seat, the boat surged forward smoothly, cutting through the small waves like a blade. The speed was impressive. The skiff seemed to be propelled by a silent, hidden engine. My friends applauded and all together implored: 'Give us a shot, give us a chance as well!'

The right to use each other's things, whether it was a bicycle or a boat, at least once, was a kind of iron rule among the lakeside clan. No, I was not keen on the idea. It was as though I were being forced to let them try my woman, one by one, but there was no escape. So I was compelled to halt my boat in the water and let them get in one after the other and, as if that were not enough, to teach each of them how to control it and make the seat move so as to obtain maximum advantage in rowing. To put up with their shouts of joy and to stand by as they inevitably overturned the boat, which had then to be lifted out of the water, emptied and dried out, was for me the equivalent of being scourged.

At the end of it all, I was left alone with my skiff once again in my arms. I lifted it up and, carrying it on my head like the god of the Amazons, I almost ran home, fearful that those idiots would follow me with shouts of: 'Come back! Give us another shot!'

On the beach along from the bridge where we would go to bathe, there were whole family groups evacuated because of the bombing. Among that colony of strangers, it was impossible not to notice two stupendous girls, both more or less fourteen years old. The one had locks of dark, curly hair, the other had blonde, straight hair. The two friends ran and jumped about in and out of the water, laughing and showing off two elegant, slim bodies in a non-stop mannequin parade.

Each one of us gawked at them, alternating between moments of wonder and flushes of heat, but we were taken aback by their behaviour: it was as if we were not there. To get ourselves noticed, we threw ourselves off the mooring masts which jutted out of the water and made a flashy display with pirouetting dives, but those two strangers did not deign to pay us any attention. They were often on their own, especially in the water, where they swam with perfect style: arm and leg breast-stroke movements that would have graced any competition . . . that is, they dipped of sight under the water level to reappear with a scissors-kick of the legs.

We were not inferior as regards style, and in particular we knew perfectly well the movement of the currents and how to take advantage of them to have ourselves carried along more quickly.

Of the two, the one who attracted me more was Lucy, with her dark, curly hair. I managed to speak to her for a moment in the water. She and Jute, her friend of German origin, had ventured very far out. Taking advantage of a current parallel to the direction they had taken, I caught up with them and warned them: 'Careful, you're right in the middle of a cold current. You could get cramp. I'd advise you to shift over a few strokes in the direction of the mountain, where I've come from. The current there is warmer and it helps you to move more quickly.'

Both of them smiled and thanked me, especially Lucy, who came over to me and asked how to work out the direction and quality of the currents. I could not believe that I was being given the chance to display my knowledge as scientist of the lakelands. I felt like the complete master of the waters!

She even paid me a compliment: 'You have a fine style of entry into the water. Who taught you?'

'I learned here on the lake, watching those who are good at it.' I would have liked to say something gracious to her as well, but I was as dumbstruck as a pickled perch.

Back on shore, we said goodbye to each other, and I did not see her for a week. Perhaps she had gone to a different beach, perhaps she had left. A few days later, I wandered along the pathway dug into the cliffside above the lime kilns further along the coast. Down below, in a kind of green harbour, there was someone playing in the water. I recognised her at once: it was her, in the company of young man with whom she was skylarking. He was diving under water and tossing her up in the air; both were laughing uproariously. A few paces more and

I was standing on a kind of balcony above them. She caught sight of me, and gave me a faint wave. Her friend pushed her underwater, and she came bouncing back to the surface, but as she thrashed about, legs flailing, she unintentionally gave him a sharp kick on the male reproductive bits and pieces. The lad let out a piercing scream, and I could not help exploding in laughter. Lucy, too, burst out laughing, but he shot me a look of undying hatred.

A few days later, it was the feast of the *Calend de Magg*, May Day. On top of Mount Domo, the peasants had planted a flowering tree. It was an ancient rite, still called, in Tuscany, the *Piantar maggio*, the Planting of May. A long pole whose top was decorated with peach, apple and cherry shoots and covered with newly blossoming flowers was driven into the ground. The Fascists did not take kindly to this rite, in part because for almost half a century the *Piantar maggio* was also a celebration of Labour Day, but the regime turned a blind eye to it and let folk get on with it. It was a lovely day. There was not a ripple on the lake as I set off in my boat, pushing gently, with no great effort, towards the island of Cannero where stood the ruins of the Malpaga Castle, named after the famous pirate brothers who had built it in the sixteenth century. I was almost at the centre of the lake when I became aware of someone swimming a little ahead of me. This person was doing a harmonious crawl, well up to competition standard, and bobbed in and out of the water. She shook her long, black hair. It was her, Lucy! I greeted her, and she turned, smiling but surprised.

'Don't you think it's bit risky to come so far out on your own?'

'Don't worry, Jute and her brother will be along in a moment to pick me up on their motorboat. I dived in ten minutes ago. They're going to the island and they'll be here any time now.'

'If you like, I'll stop and wait for them with you.'

'No,' she said, abruptly, 'thank you but I prefer to be on my own . . . forgive me.' And she started off, dipping her face into the water at every stroke. I continued on my way, sinking the oars deep into the water. I moved off, mortified and more than a little offended. 'Who does she think she is, this stuck-up, conceited so-and-so? "No, thank you but I prefer to be on my own!"'

It was the first time a girl had spoken down to me in that way. Whereas the others, they . . . ? It was not that I had girl-friends.

I looked out at the island with the castle to see if there was any sign of the motorboat, but there was nothing to be seen. On the other side, behind the headland along the coast, I noticed a black line running along the bottom of the lake.

'Madonna!' I exclaimed, 'that's the sign that the *inverna* wind is getting up, which means there'll be a storm. It'll be on us in less than twenty minutes . . . and those imbeciles on the motorboat are not even on the horizon!' I stopped rowing and turned the boat round. I went at breakneck speed towards the centre of the lake, caught up with Lucy who was now agitated and in difficulty.

'Lucky you came back,' she shouted to me. 'I'm getting cramp.'

'Take it easy, I'll help you onto the boat.'

'Thanks, but what is that black strip down there?'

'It's a fierce squall.'

'Does that mean a hurricane?'

'Yes, but relax. There's time enough before it hits us. But come on, get up here! There's only one system to stop the boat from capsizing. We've got to do the crossbar balance.'

'What does that mean?'

'I'll explain to you as we go. I stretch out full-length, side-ways . . . like that, with my bottom on one side and my back propped against the other . . . perfect! Now I put my legs in the water, feet first, being careful to keep my balance, just like a set of scales . . . you see? Now you sit astride my feet . . . come on! Try to move up to my knees. Well done. Now see if you can slide forward on your front, holding onto the side of the skiff with both hands. Careful, now I'll raise my legs very slowly until I can pull you on top of me. Like that, that's it!'

I give Lucy a push and she flies into the boat with a cry. Her body was completely on top of mine, leaving us in an embrace: she laughed, I was out of breath. I would have stayed that way forever, but the wind was starting to howl menacingly. I turned her over gently, making her take a seat in the shell of the skiff. I took up the oars and started rowing in an attempt to get away from the swelling waves. The first gusts hit the boat, hurling flurries of foam over us. I decided to head for the port in Cannero, so as to get the wind at my back. We made it into the mouth of the port just in time to escape the first heavy blasts of the squall, and were swept powerfully onto the low bank. The boat slid bodily up the beaten-earth slope. 'If I'd had to wait for my friends' boat, I'd definitely have gone under like a stone,' commented Lucy. 'What can have happened to them?'

Among the people on the shoreline cheering us on, there was someone I knew, a schoolfriend of mine called Aristide. Lucy was trembling and could hardly stand. I too was exhausted, but like the valiant saviour I was, I lifted her in my arms. 'Come over here,' shouted Aristide, 'let's go into this bar.' I took a couple of paces, and instantly my legs gave way. Two youths grabbed hold of me before I landed on top of the girl. My friend undertook to carry Lucy, and they moved smartly towards the bar. 'Hey,' I shouted, 'and what about me? Are you abandoning me here like some poor son-of-a-bitch?' It was all I could do, crawling on all fours, to make it on my own to the bar. They brought out a blanket and put it over me.

'I can't see Lucy. Where is she?'

'The woman took her up to her bathroom for a hot shower.'

I asked if they had any news about a motorboat which should have berthed before the squall blew up. 'Yes,' they replied, 'There is one which has docked down at the police jetty. It had broken down, the engine was completely seized up.'

Aristide appeared at the door and pointed out over the lake directly in front of him. 'They're taking the two strangers, the girl's friends, over to the far side of the lake. Look, they're circling round the spot where you were a little while ago. Obviously they don't know you reached land.' Aristide picked up the telephone and dialled the number of the police station. Someone needed to tell the people in the motor launch that the girl had been brought ashore. Aristide put down the receiver and said: 'Everything's OK. Unfortunately the launch can't turn back to pick you up. With the waves whipped up by the squall, it might get battered onto the coast. They're heading for the far side, where they'll be able to shelter in Germignana Bay.'

In the bar, Lucy was now in tears on a chair, releasing all the accumulated tension of our adventure. She was worried about her mother who wouldn't have seen her return, so I made an attempt to calm her down. 'Don't worry, I asked Aristide to get the policemen to let your parents know you're safe and well.'

'But you don't even know where I live.'

'Oh yes, I do. Villa Mainer, Castelvecchia, care of the Unner family . . .'

'But look . . . how did you find all that out?'

'I've been spying on you. I crept up on you a couple of days ago. I know everything about you. You have a sister and a grandfather, your mother's from Milan and your father's from Hungary and he's a dentist.' She laughed, untroubled.

By now, the big breakers from the lake were battering ferociously against the facade of the bar. The owners pulled the shutters down and reinforced the doors and windows from the inside with heavy tables. Still wrapped up in blankets, we went out by the back door with Aristide as our guide, and made for his house higher up, beyond the headland. Her mother greeted us with great warmth. When her son explained the dangers we had faced, she was close to tears. She took Lucy in her arms and hugged her. When she realised that under the blanket, the girl was wearing nothing but a wet costume, she took her by the hand upstairs to the bedrooms. I went with Aristide to his room and he gave me some dry clothes.

A short time later, we all sat down at table. The Signora took my hand in hers and then, looking at Lucy, asked: 'You're engaged, aren't you?'

There was a moment of embarrassed silence, then Lucy took charge: 'Yes, since this spring.'

'Ha, ha!' the Signora laughed. 'Look at your boyfriend blushing! There's nothing to be ashamed of, son. If you don't fall in love at your age, when will you?'

After supper, the Signora took us to our two respective bedrooms. 'You're too young to sleep in the same bed!' was her comment. 'I'm sure your mother would never forgive me.' Lucy smiled.

We retired. I lay down on the big bed, but I couldn't get to sleep. Outside, the howls of the wind, as it twisted along the canal, were punctuated by the crash of uprooted trees. Lightning, followed by claps of thunder which sounded like explosions in a mine shaft, lit up the sky. A particularly terrible gust blew open the windows. I rose to fasten it, but struggled to get it closed. I turned round and in the doorway stood Lucy, clutching a blanket.

'I'm so afraid,' she said. 'Can I stay here with you?'

I muttered something incomprehensible and made her a sign to come in. She went straight to the bed and sat down. After a brief preamble which made no sense at all, I asked her: 'I saw you once with Jute's brother. You were playing and laughing in the water . . .'

'No,' she stopped me firmly. 'He's not my boyfriend. He's very keen on me, but I don't like him.'

'Except when he plays with you in the water and throws you in the air and catches you in his arms.'

'Oh God, we're only just engaged and already you're throwing a jealous fit.' We both laughed.

'Anyway, I still have a bone to pick with you. Don't get annoyed, but can you explain why you didn't want to come with me when I caught up with you in the water?'

'It's simple. Because I didn't want Jute and her brother to see us together when they came back with their motorboat. She's always nagging at me, telling me that every time I see you I go into a flutter like a nun standing in front of a naked Saint Sebastian pierced with arrows. Not to mention her brother who's much worse. He's very jealous of you . . . to put it mildly, you give him a pain in the balls. If he'd found you and me in your yawl, tangled up in each other's arms after we tumbled in together, there was every chance he'd have rammed into you with his big, show-off motorboat.'

I was panting like a bellows, but I was also getting rid of all the bile which had built up in the pit of my stomach.

Outside, the storm roared noisily: at times it quietened down, only to begin howling again more loudly than before. We told each other everything, starting from the first time we had met on the beach. She made fun of my acrobatic diver displays, especially since more often than not they ended with horrendous belly flops. I got back at her over certain poses and attitudes she struck: I laughed, and she denied that she had ever behaved in that way.

She was clearly flattered at having produced such emotion in me. I stood up on the bed and began mimicking her various ways of walking, real mannequin parade stuff, in front of us awestruck lads, her way of running, jumping . . . I even imitated her voice and laughter. Lucy rolled about laughing, and in fact careered about on the bed so much that she fell off and landed on the floor with a great thud. 'Oh God, my head! What a bump!' I had to take hold of her to help her back to her feet. She embraced me and gave me a tiny peck on the cheek. My heart was beating in my temples, in my chest and right down to my toes. We carried on chattering, lying one close to the other, but when the first rays of light began to filter in through the shutters, it was a struggle to speak; our words came out mangled by sleepiness. We fell asleep like two children. For both of us it was first love. I was seventeen and she fourteen. Blessed be that squall!

# CHAPTER 22

## Fleeing to Switzerland

I was seventeen when the British and Americans landed in Sicily. A few months later, the Fascist government fell and the king decreed an armistice. In the immediate aftermath, many men from our neighbourhood returned home, some from Yugoslavia, others from the South of Italy. I saw one friend of mine return from Croatia dressed as a train driver, another arrive on a woman's bicycle disguised as a baker, covered in flour; yet another was done up in a strange mixture of sailor's trousers and postman's jacket.

Some days after that, I found myself in Milan, in the house of my uncle Nino, my mother's brother, who had been granted exemption from military service. He came to meet me at school. 'I need you. Perhaps you can help me.'

'Glad to. What do you need?'

'Women's wigs!'

'Wigs! What for?'

'Later. I'll explain later.'

At one end of Corso Garibaldi, there was a shop where wigs were on sale cheaply. We went there. They had about a dozen moth-eaten samples, all at bargain prices, so my uncle took the lot. 'Come with me to the station.'

When we got there he said: 'It might be a good idea if you

were to come with me to Sartirana. Maybe you could make yourself useful!'

'Just what do you plan to do with those wigs in Sartirana?'

Once we were inside the compartment, he opened the sack he had with him. Inside, all musty, there were some women's dresses. Then from a semi-rigid bag, he took out a box with make-up. 'Are you going to do a performance?' I asked.

'Almost. In Torreberretti, there's a camp with British, South African and a few Indian prisoners. The garrison that's supposed to be in charge of it has made off, so now we've got to get them to Switzerland before the Germans wake up to the fact. I have been asked to take care of about fifty of them. If I stick them all on a train in civilian clothes, they'll stand out too easily. I can hardly pass them off as people going to the Pirelli factory annual picnic! Apart from anything else, about a dozen of them are Scottish, almost all with red hair and white faces splattered with freckles. Another half a dozen are South African, one metre ninety tall, and feet that take a size fifty-four. And that's before we get to the four Indians that look like versions of the famous Tugh from Malaya!

'I don't get it, Uncle. Do you really believe that if you dress them up in wigs and make-up they could pass as a Variety chorus on the move?'

'I've not going to dress them all up, just about ten of the ones who would stick out like sore thumbs. Then we'll put them all onto the same train as the *catariso* folk.'

'And who would they be?'

'The *catariso* are the people who come to Lomellina from the city in search of a few sacks of rice, rye or wheat so that they can for once eat like human beings. The guards on the government warehouses let them get away with it, because as long as the amount does not exceed a couple of kilos a head, it's permissible. All we have to do is mix our prisoners in with the *catariso*, who are mostly women. In fact, we might even entrust some of the more passable ones to them!'

'Are you sure that these *catariso* women are prepared to take the risk?'

'Don't worry. Women are always more generous, and they're always the ones prepared to run risks.'

The following morning, when it was still dark, we went to the station at Sartirana. The train coming from Mortara for Novara and Luino arrived. It was already quite busy, mainly with *catariso* women with their bags and packages. The train stopped, took on more passengers, then, instead of moving off, reversed to the shed where it was joined to a goods train. I learned later that this manoeuvre was a ruse to allow the liberated prisoners to get onto the rear coaches undercover, in other words, to dash out from the arches in the shed, out of sight of the guards on duty in the station. Clearly the engine drivers and conductors had been squared.

I followed Uncle Nino down to the rear coaches. Four comrades from Sartirana had been put in charge of overseeing the transport. As my uncle had forecast, at least a dozen women had volunteered to take part in the adventure. Some of them were obviously completely unconcerned about any risk they might encounter. 'If we're rounded up, I want to be locked up with that good-looking Scottish guy who is disguised as a rice-gatherer!' one of the women giggled.

It was an exceptionally well-assorted gang of escapees! Almost the whole bunch were done up in trousers which were too short and tight, while those with the wigs on their heads looked like dockside whores in the middle of a particularly bothersome period of abstinence. Someone had even put a baby who was kicking and screaming in abject terror on the knees of one of those streetwalkers.

The greatest danger was that some traveller or other would ask one them a question, for not one of them had so much as a word of Italian. Of the four from the Indian subcontinent, two spoke an impenetrable Bangladeshi dialect while another was so dark of skin that not even a heavy dose of foundation cream would have lightened his complexion. Having tried everything else, they had decided to swathe his face in bandages, leaving openings for the eyes, nostrils and the mouth. To hide his hands, they had got someone to knit waiter-style gloves. If anyone asked what had happened to him, the reply was that he had been standing nearby when flames from the furnace had blown out . . . burns all over.

As luck would have it, the coach was so packed that no one was able to get on. Instead, at each stop, we leaned out of the window to suggest to people looking for a seat that they move towards the centre of the train. Even the guards who were supposed to get on at Novara and go through the two carriages where our escaping prisoners were squatting tried only once or twice to make headway through the crowd, then gave up and climbed aboard further up the train.

We arrived in Luino, the usual half-hour late. It had taken us almost four hours to do no more than one hundred kilometres.

At this point, the whole undertaking became more difficult. A garrison of Germans was waiting for us at the station, and to make matters worse, the number of travellers in our compartment had been almost halved. We could no longer take advantage of the crush to stave off the possibility of inspections. In addition, with the passage of time, the make-up cream was beginning to stream down the faces of the disguised runaways. They now looked like clowns fleeing from a custard-pie-in-the-face competition.

'Watch out, four "Deutsch" inspectors clambering aboard the rear carriages to pay us a visit!' At that moment, the train moved off, jolting so powerfully that one of the Wehrmacht men, standing with one foot on the running board, was thrown onto the ground. The station-master whistled like a madman. The train shuddered to a halt. Another jolt. The four Germans went racing up towards the locomotive. The head conductor got off to scream at the station-master: the engine driver leaned out of his cab and started screaming in his turn. The Germans tried gamely to get into the discussion, but no one paid any heed to them. As if that were not enough, the normal travellers leaned out of the windows and did their own yelling: 'We're already a half-hour late! Would you like to wind up your argy-bargy and get this train rolling again?'

The result was that the station-master cut the whole thing short with one almighty blow of his whistle, the train engine replied with a snort and set off resolutely with the indignant puffing of one who is fed up to his back teeth. The station-master on the platform continued debating the matter with the Kraut guards, and as I drew level with the altercating parties, I had the clear impression that once more the railwaymen in Luino and those on our train had set up the whole scene with the express purpose of stymying the German gendarmes and preventing them from carrying out their inspection.

After half an hour, once we were beyond Maccagno, we arrived at the tunnel a few kilometres short of Pino, that is, a few steps from the Swiss border. The train stopped with the engine and the greater part of the carriages inside the tunnel, leaving only the rear coaches outside. 'Out, down you get, off you go!'

Hardly had our feet touched the ground when the train started up again. The fifty prisoners and those of us in the escort had made it, even if we had been tossed about a bit!

Not far behind us, there was a path which led into the woods and then wended its way upwards over a steep shoulder. We climbed at the pace of wild goats. The supposedly scalded Tugh pulled the bandages off his face, and with cries of satisfaction, those who had been disguised as women stripped off their skirts and bodices. There was no time to stop and get them into trousers, and so they were obliged to remain in their underpants. The tension caused them to neglect removing their wigs . . . an ever-more obscene vision.

When we reached the plain above Tronzano, we ran into a group of shepherds – men and women – and at the sight of the various Tughs, African giants, fair-skinned, red-haired Scots and striding women, they opened wide their startled eyes; the women made the sign of the cross. A few more paces and we were on the frontier. We stopped at a hut to get a drink and catch our breath. There waiting for us were a couple of smugglers whom I had known for years, as well as another group of people, men, women and children. In the middle of them, I saw my father, who had come up with the people from Pino. I had not expected to see him up there. We embraced and he complimented Uncle Nino and his companions: 'You had some courage to make him do a journey like that!'

Two peasant women emerged from the hut to hand out slices of cheese and polenta. A shepherd came up with some flasks of wine, and milk for the children. I asked my father: 'Who are these people you brought with you?'

'Jews,' he replied. 'That's now the third group we've brought over in the past few days. Anyway, I'll have to be saying goodbye to you, because I've to be back in an hour to go on duty at the station.'

Before he set off, he went over to speak to the fleeing Jews. Each one embraced him. As he made his way over the ridge, they all shouted their thanks and good wishes.

The Britons there asked Uncle Nino about that man whom everyone was cheering with such warmth. They were told he was in charge of the organisation responsible for bringing the persecuted and escapees to Switzerland. They, too, then cheered him.

My father, further down, gave a wave of his arm and continued his descent. I was very proud of him.

# CHAPTER 23

## Voluntary Conscription

The war was coming to an end, even if it was still causing mourning and tragedy. I was beginning to believe that, although there had been some heart-stopping moments when I had escaped only by the skin of my teeth, I had been successful in steering clear of it and avoiding any real trouble.

In Milan, I had the misfortune to be caught in one of the heaviest bombing raids the city had seen. I was lodging with an aunt in Isola, an old quarter behind the Garibaldi district. She had been evacuated to Brianza and had left me the keys of her flat, but that evening I had not made it back from Corso Buenos Aires, where I happened to be. I was getting onto a tram when the alarm sounded and I had to go down into the shelter under the Teatro Puccini. In no time, it seemed as though the end of the world was upon us: plaster flakes and dust rained down on us at every blast. The bombing lasted several hours, with only a few breaks. When the sirens gave the all-clear, we all trooped out and, as the smoke dispelled, we were faced with a horrendous spectacle: buildings in flames, blocks of flats reduced to rubble, piles of debris blocking the streets, emergency vehicles unable to find a way though and fire-brigade sirens screaming on all sides. I saw all around me blank, uncomprehending faces, and I doubt if mine was any different.

There was no way through that infernal labyrinth of twisted metal and wreckage, until finally I stumbled across a boy guiding a Red Cross ambulance, and he showed me how to get out.

The sun was high in the sky when I got back to Isola: same disaster, same acrid, throat-burning smoke caused by the phosphorous bombs.

I made my way to the street where I was lodging: my aunt's house was at the foot of the street, but at the foot of that street there was nothing. The whole four-storey building had collapsed. As I stood there, I felt someone tap me on the shoulder: it was the grocer from the shop in the building opposite. 'What are you doing here? We had given you up for dead. Not a soul got out of your building alive . . .'

'Forgive me if I chose not to be on that list!'

In other words, as I said at the beginning of this story, things were going quite well for me – apart from the terror. I was seventeen and a half, and the end of the war could not be too far off. The Allies had reached the so-called Gothic Line in the Apennines. A few months more and they would overrun it. I was not due to be drafted for more than a year, so I was covered.

But instead the Salò government devised a cunning trick to trap all of us lads not due to be called up immediately. Without warning, they issued an edict requiring all those born in the early months of 1926 to present themselves for dispatch to work in Germany. In the small print, they explained that we would be employed mainly in factories and in useful services. In short, we were to make up for the skill shortages resulting from the disastrous bombing raids. My father's immediate comment was: 'It's worse for you all than being sent to the front!'

There was one way out: the Anti-Aircraft Artillery Command in Varese was accepting volunteers. Anyone who enlisted in that corps could avoid being sent as a pseudo-deportee to Germany. No sooner said than done: I linked up with a sizeable group of conscripts of the same age as myself, nearly all from the lakelands, and all together we presented ourselves at the artillery barracks. We were mightily pleased with our choice, not least because they assured us that, since there were no active artillery postings available, high command would send us temporarily back home, on provisional leave, pending further orders. But, alas! it was a trap: that very evening we were given a consignment of uniforms, kitbags and equipment. Very early the following morning, they loaded all thirty of us, scared little rabbits that we were, onto cattle trucks bound for Mestre, where we were to receive instruction in the use of heavy artillery. There was a sign printed in large letters on the side of the carriages transporting us – horses 12, men 40: in other words, the advantage lay with the horses. The commanding officers behaved with a certain magnanimity towards their dazed recruits: there were only thirty-five of us to each coach. What extravagance!

It was summer and the heat inside those wooden boxes was suffocating, so we travelled with the door wide open. As the train speeded up, the din and the creaking grew in volume until it left us stunned. How did the horses cope?

When we arrived in Milan, they shunted us into a siding and we got off to go in search of water. We found a fountain near a goods yard and filled our flasks. Returning to our train, we cut across five or six lines and then proceeded alongside a row of coaches, from which we heard people shouting to us: there were gaps between the wooden boards, and through them we made out eyes and mouths begging us for something to drink.

'Water, water!' repeated men, women and children. Some of our number tried to force open the doors, but they were all locked and bolted. A boy from Luino exclaimed: 'But these are deportees!'

There were some cartons lying on the ground. We cut them into strips a couple of centimetres long, then each of us stuck his narrow piece of material in between the gaps and began to pour in water which flowed along the cardboard and down on the other side of the wall, where thirsty mouths opened wide to gulp every last drop.

After a few minutes we heard the cry: '*Weg! Weg von hier! Es ist verboten!*' The German soldiers guarding the train came running up in a fury, using the butt of their rifles to shove us back.

Fortunately for us, we were saved by an officer who appeared with a detachment of around a dozen railway guards. The determination and resolve they showed silenced the bawling of the Krauts, who discreetly retired. We climbed back on our trucks. The images of despair, the imploring voices, those faces glimpsed between the bars of locked and bolted wagons would never leave our memories.

We arrived in Mestre two days later. American bombers had made a direct hit on the two bridges over the Adige, so we had to make the crossing on a barge. We were still on board, a few metres from the bank, when the alarms sounded and the rumbling of engines was heard overhead. Some, panic-stricken, dived into the water, but on this occasion the bombs were not destined for us. The four-engine planes were heading for Germany.

In the Mestre barracks, we joined another thousand or so recruits from all over Italy, the majority of whom had enlisted for the same reasons as us: to avoid forced transfer to Germany for work in factories which were being carpet-bombed. But even in that area of sea, canals and marshes, it was no laughing matter to have all those bombs raining down.

A few days after our arrival, we were evicted from the barracks and taken to the countryside, where we were billeted in various abandoned houses. We had to sleep stretched out on the beaten-earth floors. We asked an elderly sergeant why we had been moved. 'We had to make way for a battalion returning from Yugoslavia,' was the reply. That night, they bombed Mestre and Marghera. We could see flames and white flashes rising over the residential areas, and could hear the roar of the aeroplane engines as they passed over our heads. A matter of minutes later, streaks of light and tongues of fire shot up somewhere behind us. Immediately afterwards, an endless volley of terrifying blasts caused the ground to tremble. 'They're flattening Treviso,' shouted the sergeant. The anti-aircraft guns fired wildly, making it all look like a carnival fireworks display, but at that moment more than ten thousand people, men, women and children, were dying.

Today it would be called collateral damage.

But why this massacre? Were these not supposed to be our liberators? Wave after wave of bombers came over as we stood there in the fields, staring at the skies, petrified.

No sooner had the flashes and blasts ended than from the distance we heard the screech of sirens as fire engines raced out from Padua. Near to where we were standing, three roads met: one from the direction of the lagoon, another running from Mestre to Treviso, and the third snaking up from the 'Pavania', that is, the zone around Padua. The fire engines were all heading for Treviso. One vehicle pulled up in front of the house where we were lodged, and an officer got down to tell us to stand by in readiness to be moved to Mestre. They needed man-power to shift the debris and help out with the first-aid services. Minutes later, we were loaded onto lorries and taken to the city.

They had struck the entire city centre. I found myself facing the same scene as in Milan, with the one difference that huge craters had opened up and from them jets of water were shoot-ing into the air like fountains: people screaming, the wounded being carried away in the arms of helpers, the dead laid out under the porches. It was a full hour before we got ourselves organised. No one had told us what to do. Earth-moving machines with mechanical diggers arrived, and we were handed spades and told to pile up the debris pushed aside by the bulldozers. We heard voices from underneath slabs of stone, and hacked furiously at the rubble until a kind of tunnel opened up: little by little, one by one, we pulled about ten people out. Our hands were bleeding: only a few of us could boast the hard, callused skin of building-workers.

Next day, parade in the central barracks, change of uniform. 'The clothes you are wearing are winter gear, you'll die in this heat, but we've managed to get you more suitable uniforms, summer wear.' They distributed strangely coloured trousers and jackets, the yellow of desert sand. We put them on, and stared at each other wide-eyed. 'But these are German uniforms, Wehrmacht uniforms!'

'Don't talk nonsense,' the officers reassured us. 'They may be German but the insignia is our army's. Calm down.'

In the following days, we began training: 'We'll do a little practice with these model-88 cannons.'

'But aren't they the ones we borrowed from the German anti-aircraft divisions?'

'We'll have to adapt and work with their batteries. Our own model-91 guns are not available at the moment.'

A week went by. Another parade. 'Pack up your kits, gather your things together. You're going home, or at least to Monza, the HQ of the four battalions. We'll continue our training exercises there, since that camp is better equipped.'

We got back aboard the goods coaches, together with the veterans from Yugoslavia. One of them commented: 'I can't see anything good coming from this transfer. I think they're going to fuck us good and proper.'

'In what way?' we recruits asked.

'In what way, I couldn't say, but this business of the Deutsch uniforms . . . the training with the Kraut model-88, and now this transfer with an escort of German guards . . . doesn't smell good.'

'Where are these Kraut guards?' we asked incredulously.

'Just wait. They'll be along any moment.'

I have no idea how the 'old hands' had got wind of it, but the moment we got settled in the goods carriages, along came our guardian angels, armed with machine guns and Gerver rifles. They took up position in the conductor's cabin, without so much as deigning to glance at us. 'Don't get upset,' advised a sergeant, 'they're here to protect us.'

'From what? From the big, bad wolf?'

As the train drew in to Verona, the sirens, as punctual as bad luck, were going off. The engineers had only just replaced the destroyed bridge with another one supported on pontoons. Our troop train pulled up about a hundred metres from the new bridge, the doors were thrown open and we jumped down from the coaches. 'Leave your kitbags on the train: they'll only get in the way,' shouted the sergeants.

I did not understand why all the old hands ignored that advice and dragged their bags along with them. The order was to stand back from the banks of the Adige and away from the railway line. 'Spread out in the fields, in the middle of the corn, but stay together,' yelled the German interpreter, obviously a native of Alto Adige.

'He's off his head,' we all guffawed as one. 'How can you spread out and stay together?' Our laughter quickly died away, or more precisely froze in our throats. About half a dozen Hurricanes were nose-diving towards us, dropping bombs as though they were handfuls of rice scattered over newly-weds. At each raid, jets of water and gravel were tossed up into the air.

'Got it dead-centre!' was the cry of one of our men as he peeped out from the shoots of wheat, but in fact as the clouds of dust created by the explosion cleared away, the bridge floating on the pontoons came back into view, rocking uncertainly after the buffeting it had taken, but perfectly intact. That bridge seemed magic! After the third unsuccessful attack, the Hurricane squadron gave up and retired to their base behind the Gothic Line. 'All clear! Back on the train.'

Several of the carriages seemed to have been holed, as one of the American hunter jets had been firing twenty-millimetre rounds at the train. So that was why the veterans from Yugoslavia had taken their kit and belongings with them!

At this point, the sergeants of the various companies began to take the roll-call, but our officer in charge was no longer there. The Germans in the escort started swearing: *Hurensohne! Fanhfluchtige! Verrate!* It was not long before we discovered the reason for this rage. All the more experienced members of the detachment, including our sergeant, had made off. Disappeared!

We set off again. The carriage we were travelling in was one of those which had been holed, and many of the kitbags had been ripped apart. The Germans ordered us off yet again: the train was about to cross the bridge, but it was too risky for us to stay on board. The troop made the crossing on foot, hopping from one plank to the other. Finally we got back into our trucks, and here we had the joy of a wholly unexpected surprise: as we took our place in the carriage, the German escort slammed the doors shut, locking us in with padlocks. 'What's going on? Are we being deported now?' we yelled in indignation. 'Bastards!'

The interpreter, with his rich Bolzano accent, shouted back at us: 'Say your prayers that they don't come back and bomb us again, because this time no one's getting off. You're staying put! You've got your son-of-a-bitch friends who took to their heels to thank for that!' We stayed on our feet in those creaking traps, totally bemused by what was going on, while the train sped along at high speed. A couple of hours without further mishap and we were at the Sesto San Giovanni junction outside Milan: another half-hour and we finally reached Monza.

A completely peaceful week followed, making us more than ever convinced that the veterans' flight had been a futile and risky act, leaving them liable to arrest and arraignment in front of a court martial on a charge of desertion in the face of the enemy. Meanwhile, every day, other artillery contingents arrived from Albania and Greece, each group escorted by men from the Wehrmacht. From time to time, some soldiers from the SS would turn up, but there was nothing to fear. Apart from anything else, those of us who were enrolled at the university had no problem obtaining permission to go to Milan to take our exams. So it was that every week I went to the *Accademia della*

*Brera* to continue work on my thesis, and to the *Politecnico* to do the so-called 'Six Days', a practical examination involving a survey of historic buildings. In the barracks, I kept myself busy doing portraits of various non-commissioned officers in the battalion. I admit it: a classic example of beguiling arse-licking, winning me the privilege of wandering from office to office and of obtaining for myself concessions and special leave. In all honesty, my life in those barracks in Monza was almost idyllic. Slowly, the nightmare of the journey on the troop train as deportees was slipping away from my mind: even the Germans had disappeared. The Mestre episode, the carpet-bombing, the job of digging out corpses now seemed to all of us like a distant memory, better forgotten. The final, definitive liberation from that nightmare was the order for a further change of uniform. In truth, I would be tempted to describe it as the ultimate metamorphosis, for this rite also involved the transformation of our physical role in the whole absurd comedy. The order to change clothing and role was imparted to us in the course of a parade in which we were introduced to the new commander-in-chief of the anti-aircraft artillery. No sooner were we lined up on the big parade-ground than a gruff but extremely personable colonel appeared, gave a summary glance at us then almost assaulted us: 'What is this God-awful costume they've dressed you up in? That's the yellow of dromedary shit, all very well for the desert. Very sorry for the lot of you, but the Afrika Korps has been disbanded! Kaput! So, either you find yourselves a camel each, or else ditch that uniform!' There was a general guffaw, and even a sprinkling of applause. That wit and outrageous irony from an officer were liberating bombshells.

He was as good as his word. Dispatched back to our quarters, shoved as naked as spawning worms through showers, having a whale of a time in a joyous parade of quivering privates of sizes and shapes to suit all tastes, we were finally issued with new uniforms. They did nothing to enhance our virile, war-like appearance, and indeed quite suddenly we once again took on our natural aspect of pathetic Italian rookies: a sign that we really were back home again!

Urged on by men from my own part of the world, I resumed my habit of putting on performances of my comic stories. I had begun working on a new repertoire based on our less than pleasurable experiences at Mestre, episodes which my fellows and I had lived through personally but which we had almost completely erased. One which went down particularly well was the story of the rescue of the Mestre streetwalkers. These poor, piece-work Vestal non-Virgins had been buried alive when their 'red house', the little villa on the outskirts of the city where they operated, had collapsed. Their numbers, granted the vicinity of barracks filled with troops groaning under the pain of long-term abstinence, were considerable: around fifty devotees of the multiple orgasm. On the famous night when it was completely destroyed, the house of phallic relief was literally overflowing with guests anxious to free their loins of the troublesome accumulation of seminal liquid. When the sirens went off, not one of them so much as entertained the prudent idea of evacuating the premises. The Madame, with all due zeal, advised the assembled clients to make themselves comfortable in the well-furnished, underground cellars, but would you believe it, not a single one among them paid heed. As the old scientific adage has it: 'The erect penis often indicates a complete prick.' But when the first bombs began to rain down on the fun-loving band, causing explosions of such violence that the entire roof of the building was lifted clean off, the whole bunch – revellers and revelled alike – made a headlong dash for the cellars in the hope of saving their skins from the more than imminent collapse. A further blast caused all three floors to fold inexorably in on themselves like sand castles.

Our company of improvised aid-workers was first on the scene: the poor souls had been buried alive for more than an hour. For us this was the second first-aid operation – we were first, but not really operational!

An enormous earth-moving machine arrived and we set to work at once. After hours of gruelling work, we were literally drained when, all of a sudden, we heard shouting from down below: it seemed to be women's voices, and the appeals were desperate. 'Hurry up with those bloody shovels! Get a move on with the bulldozer! We're suffocating down here.' Untrained bunglers though we were, the urgency of the impending tragedy spurred us on, but we only succeeded in throwing heaps of rubble over one another. To make matters worse, groups of curious individuals gathered around the collapsed building, each one lavish with advice but unwilling to lend a hand.

I somehow got into a cavity in the middle of the debris outside a jammed door. I shouted to them to pass me down a pickaxe or sledge hammer. I was handed the implement, raised it up, flexed my muscles and brought it down with all the force I could muster. The door fell in cleanly and a half-naked girl appeared out of the dust: when she caught sight of me, she leaped forward, laughing, crying and shouting, then gave me a hug and a big kiss on the mouth. The woman behind her pushed her out of the way, and she too gave me a full, open-mouthed kiss, sticking her tongue down my throat and spinning it around like a roller, leaving me quite out of breath. Thank God my first-aid companions were there to pull me away from the entrance and generously take my place, receiving in their turn the passionate hugs and kisses offered in grateful recompense by the liberated women. Something of a traffic jam was created by the pushes and changes-of-guard among the helpers, each one anxious to claim his portion of the gratitude. One late-comer, desirous of his fair share of kisses, came on the scene just as a naked German soldier was exiting: he gave him a slobbering, double dose of lips-on-the-mouth, with the accompanying movements of the tongue. The violated victim mechanically went for his holster to pull out his gun: luckily for the kisser, the enraged Teuton was completely naked!

My tale was met with gales of raucous laughter which rose and fell with a rhythmically perfect crescendo, reaching its peak with the scene of the naked women emerging to freedom, offering their liberators their gift of tits, mouths and round buttocks. The finale of the German soldier, mouth filled with Italian tongue, was greeted by the audience with extremely warm applause. Among the spectators was a corporal who howled with laughter throughout and exploded with delight at the closing sequence. When I first heard his laugh, I was taken aback. It was such an absurd guffaw that I thought he was having me on, so much so that I turned towards him and threatened: 'Watch out, Mr Corporal, because if you carry on yelping like a coyote, I'll come over and stuff my tongue so far down your throat that you'll drown.' He replied with an even more riotous burst of laughter, so I concluded that that must be his natural laugh. At the end of the performance he got up and came over to me. From his awkwardness and from the fact that he was not able to look me in the eye, I realised he was blind. 'I can't thank you enough for these side-splitting laughs you've given us. We blind people devour these fantastic images.'

I was overcome with embarrassment, I had no idea what to say but he rescued me from my awkwardness with another guffaw: 'For God's sake, it occurred to me that if I could tell stories the way you do, I could pass myself off as some kind of Homer for these shitty times.'

Later, he himself told me how he had lost his sight. During a bombing raid in Turin, a shower of debris had struck him full in the face. 'And to think that my nickname was *Bellosguardo*, 'Handsomeface'. In a few days I have to undergo another operation which hopefully will restore my sight, at least partially. I'm from Brindisi and have no relatives or friends here in the North. I've to go to the hospital and wait my turn, on my own, like an abandoned dog, and blind into the bargain. Who makes me go through with all this? The only friends I have are here in the barracks, so I'll just wait until they come for me.'

A short time later, I found out that they had given Bellosguardo a job as switchboard operator, and I went to visit him in his office. He recognised me immediately from my voice, and made a great fuss over me. He then asked me to take him to the canteen. I took him by the arm, and on the way over he said to me: 'I needed to talk to you privately, and over there in the office there's always at least one person eavesdropping. This morning with Giovanni, the recruit who's looking after me, I popped out of the barracks . . . I can come and go as I please. I had an appointment in Milan for a series of preparatory tests for the operation. Once we were inside the city walls, Giovanni alerted me to the fact that there were three or four armoured cars and a much bigger number of trucks carefully concealed among the plane trees and beeches in the park. I might be wrong, but something major is about to take place!' Bellosguardo was not in the slightest wrong. The Yugoslavia veterans, too, had got wind of the same thing when they took to their heels, for they had sensed that the Germans and the overlords in the Republic of Salò were setting a trap.

The first warning arrived exactly one day later when we discovered that all leave, including leave already requested and granted for those who had exams to do, had been cancelled. No exit from the barracks! That same day, the parade call was sounded: everyone on the parade ground in rows of three, every company to be in readiness for review. 'Look up there on the turrets,' muttered one of the sergeants, 'the Germans are positioning heavy machine guns.'

The regimental band, too, was being lined up when around a hundred SS men, armed as though for battle, came running in. The band struck up the regimental march, and from somewhere at the back German and Italian officers came forward, followed by a company of the Black Brigades. In the middle of them was Mussolini . . . yes, Mussolini himself, in uniform as in photographs from years before. He was pinched and drawn as he paraded before us, giving an occasional salute with his outstretched arm. Close up, he appeared even more emaciated and tired. He carried out the inspection, then mounted a podium hurriedly prepared with some planks, and addressed us through a microphone. There was no emphasis in his tone: 'The cities of Germany are being attacked every day and every night by enemy bombers. The civilian losses are huge, but there are also reports of losses among the units which succeed day after day in bringing down hundreds of the attackers' aircraft. The German anti-aircraft force is foremost among these heroic combatants. You will, all of you, have the great honour of joining with them to inflict a sacred lesson on the enemy, and of displaying the most tangible solidarity with an allied nation and with the German people!'

'They've stuck it up us and no mistake,' was the semi-audible comment of the commander of the battery, while the SS and the Black Brigades applauded and screamed the usual hosannas exalting death and glory. The faces of several men were lined with tears.

Mussolini and his escort exited at the same speed as they had entered. The Germans remained on the turrets with their 20-millimetre guns aimed inwards. They feared not an attack but a mutiny.

Thanks to my friend Bellosguardo, who lent me a telephone, I was able to get in touch with my father at the Pino station. 'We leave tomorrow under guard in a troop train. The city we're destined for? Maybe Dusseldorf or Dresden. If you ask me, they'll bolt the carriages shut, like the last time.'

My father was silent for a few moments, then he said: 'Whatever happens, don't lose heart. Good humour and irony are your salvation, don't ever forget that. I'm stuck here tomorrow, but Mamma will come and see you.'

Next morning, outside the barracks, there were hundreds of people, the relatives, mothers, fathers, wives and sisters of the soldiers about to depart. All of us were lined up with our bags on the parade ground, one company behind the other. The same, familiar roll-calls were being repeated, the usual insufferable rigmarole. Our detachment had been put at the end of the procession. The Colonel came over in our direction, accompanied by a sergeant who handed me a note. I glanced at it: it was from my mother. She told me she was outside, under the big beech tree. 'When you come out to get into the truck, look over this way.'

I did not see my mother that day on account of an unforeseen event. She, as she said in her note, had been standing for hours under the big tree which in dialect has the same name as me (in Lombard dialect, a beech tree is called a *fo*.). She saw companies of boys passing in front of her, desperately searching for their loved ones among the noisy, jostling throng which was held back by the German guards and by a force of around a hundred *carabinieri*, I later learned that as she stood there against the trunk of the *fo*, she suddenly heard someone whisper in her ear: 'He's not going, your boy's not going!'

A somewhat elderly woman, totally unknown to her, was at her side, leaning on the same tree. 'Were you talking to me? About my son?' she asked.

'Yes, your son . . . he's staying put!' she repeated, speaking in the dialect of Lomellina. 'He's not leaving.'

'What do you mean, not leaving? Look over there, they're all leaving, more than a thousand of them.'

'But the ones at the back are staying here.' So saying, she made off, supporting herself on her walking stick. She disappeared, swallowed up by the host of mothers running over towards another departing division.

'Signora Giuseppina Fo.' She heard her name being called out. 'Which one of you is the mother of Dario Fo? Make yourself known.'

'Me, it's me. I'm here.' She moved away from the others, still unaware of where the call was coming from.

At that moment, a soldier, or rather two soldiers, came forward, the one holding the other's arm. One of the two was blind. 'Signora Giuseppina, I have a message on behalf of your son. His company is not leaving, for the reason that they are new recruits, not fully trained in artillery techniques and the Germans don't know what to do with them.'

My mother could not speak. She embraced Corporal Bellosguardo. Other mothers who had heard the message requested more precise information.

'My son's a new recruit as well.'

'So is mine.'

'Then set your minds at peace. They're staying here,' insisted the blind corporal. 'Those who have not received training will be staying at home.'

Dozens of arms stretched out to take Bellosguardo by the hand. 'Thank you, thank you. God save you. May Jesus Christ bless you, my son!'

Bellosguardo replied: 'Well, if you see him around, put in a good word for me. See if he'll work a real miracle tomorrow!'

# CHAPTER 24

## Desertion and Escape

There are periods in the life of a man which slip away leaving no trace in his mind, others which, however brief they may be, leave deep marks on the memory, causing each moment to be imprinted as though sculpted on stone. We owe this simple intuition to a 'story-teller', Jonathan Swift by name, author of *Gulliver's Travels*, and it conveys perfectly what was happening to me in those days.

When I think back to that time between 1944 and 1945, it seems to me impossible that I lived through so many stories, all piled one on top of the other in such a brief space of time. Grotesque or tragic situations, often lived as though in a nightmare. Even today in sleep, I find myself carried painfully back to the bedlam of the bombing raids. The troop trains with the goods trucks in which I am enclosed, the escapes, the desertions, the police searching for me from village to village, all come flooding back to me. And each time, I relive the anxiety of being captured and thrown in jail. But coming back to the reality of those days, the sequence of such episodes underwent an incredible acceleration the moment the last contingent departed for Germany. The only ones left in that enormous barracks were us, the new recruits, a few elderly officers and a dozen or so sergeants. There were four hundred of us in total. A month later, my friend, Bellosguardo, who had partially regained his sight after the operation on his eyes, came to give me a piece of advice. I was in a dormitory room chatting with a friend, Marco Bianchi from Besnate, with whom only a few months previously I had been training for the four hundred metres sprint on the track at the Gallarate Sports Club. Our miracle man interrupted us: 'Watch out! In a couple of weeks they're going to pack you off too, for the same destination, Dusseldorf.'

'What do you mean? First they tell us we're useless recruits that they couldn't do anything with in Germany, and now they've changed their minds?'

'Well, you might come in handy as support staff for the artillery. You could do your apprenticeship on the job. With the carpet-bombing underway, you'd learn all the faster . . . unless you get blown apart first.'

'Bloody marvellous! We've got our arse in parsley again!' burst out Marco Bianchi, and I added: 'Hell, what a cock-up! Is there a way out this time?'

'Get the hell out! Desert,' was Bellosguardo's advice.

'Desert!'

'Yes, but cover your backsides. I mean, get yourselves a cushier number with a safer corps.'

'Which one?'

'The paratroopers at the Tradate training school. Look, in this folder there's a pamphlet asking for people to join up. They're looking for volunteers to go on the paras' course, nose to the wheel for forty days until you get the licence. One of our guys, Sergeant Paludetti, applied last month and they accepted him on the spot. That way, he managed to avoid the move to Dusseldorf.'

'OK, it went all right for him, but suppose they take one look at us, turn us down flat and throw us back into the arms of the Germans? That would really be great!'

'Yes, it's a risk, but it's the only card you have in your hand. If everything goes well and they take you on at Tradate, you're in the clear for at least another month and a half, and nothing can happen to you meantime. This bollocks of a situation has to end sometime! The British and the Americans can't stay behind the Gothic Line forever. They'll have to decide to get on with it, otherwise what kind of liberators are they?'

'All right,' the two of us accepted almost in unison, 'let's put in this damned application for the course in Tradate and be done with it.'

'By the way, will we be expected to throw ourselves out of an aeroplane?' asked Bianchi, and I came out with the comment, 'Damnation, I never thought of that!'

'Listen,' the miracle-worker cut off further discussion, 'if you feel your buttocks tightening at the idea of jumping into mid-air with a parachute, the only alternative is to ask a convent for hospitality: just up the road, you'll find the convent of the Nun of Monza, and who knows, you might even have some kind of erotic thrill thrown in.'

'All right, you've made up our minds for us. Let's write this application.'

'Application for the paratroopers or the convent?'

'Yeah, very funny.'

'In any case, my advice is not to send this letter by mail: it's better to hand it over in person.'

'Why?'

'What's wrong with you? Do you trust the mail? In this situation, in the state we're in, the application might get to Tradate on the day the war ends. And anyway, once you're actually at the training school, they might take you on there and then!'

At that moment, the trumpet call for grub sounded, and Marco and I went off to the canteen. We managed to find a table in a quiet spot. He confided: 'You know, ever since they packed us off here to Monza, I've been thinking of hightailing it: first, I was thinking of heading for Switzerland, of slipping over the border even if it means getting shot at by the Krauts. But then I discovered that for the last six months the Swiss frontier guards have been tossing people out like old brooms: they won't let anyone in any more. I even thought of joining the partisans, but after the last round-up, nearly all the groups have retreated above inaccessible peaks, like Alta Val Sesia, beyond the Scopello pass.

'So we're like rats in a trap, where the only exit opens on to a void. We've no option but to jump and hope that at least the parachute opens!'

'Our friend Bellosguardo says we should get moving at once.'

'Yes, and all things considered, it'd be better to post our enlistment applications and take a copy with us, duly stamped by our regiment.'

'Come on, do you really think the officers are going to endorse our applications?'

'Well, we have devious ways of making them do what we want.'

'But the whole thing would be thrown out by the Germans. They're the real bosses in the camp now, and if everything is not signed and sealed by them, we're done for.'

'Exactly, so what then?'

Bellosguardo appeared behind us, and interrupted in his no-nonsense way: 'Relax, you're going to get your passes.'

'But how?'

'Forge them!'

'So who's going to do it?'

The miracle worker gave me a slap on the back: 'No time for false modesty. I've seen how you churn out forged seals and stamps, you're a real master.'

'I've seen them too. You did some for me!' Bianchi testified.

'Not so fast! What you're talking about were stamps printed on passes for evening leave. No sergeant on guard duty was going to stand there poring over them. But in this case, in addition to our own official ones, I'd also need to forge Wehrmacht stamps, as well as the Krauts' signatures.'

Marco took me by the shoulder and gave me a shake: 'My dear boy, look me in the eye. It's true that if they find we're hopping it with forged documents, they'll throw us in jail and put us on trial for attempted desertion. And the chances are that at the next round of reprisals, they'll put us up against a wall with the other folk they're going to shoot. So do you think for one moment that if I were not more than certain you could do it, I'd be betting my skin on your abilities as a forger?'

He had me cornered. Bellosguardo got hold of pre-printed forms with our applications already typed out: 'The undersigned requests transfer to the Parachute School at Tradate . . .' etc.

'Hold on one moment! If I am to reproduce the concentric circles you need for the stamps, I need some metal tops from small and medium-sized jars. Then, obviously, I'm going to need a few original documents, even if they're out of date, with all the various headings and signatures.' I set to work, crushed the lead of a copying pencil to a fine dust, added a few drops of alcohol, mixed them together and . . . hey presto! an excellent forger's dye.

I took a couple of very fine sable brushes from my box of water colours, and set to work. The first stamp that came out was a mess: my fingers were sweating . . . I put my hands under cold water and tried again. The second stamp might have done, but it was not yet perfect. At the fifth attempt, I pulled it off: a masterpiece! 'Better than the original!' my two satisfied admirers commented.

I could not sleep that night. When finally I managed to drop off, I found myself playing the lead role in a terrifying nightmare. The German guards had uncovered the fraud, had collared us and were dragging us over to a wall. They fired at us with a twenty-bore machine gun, then took us to hospital. We were covered with bullet holes, but still alive. They extracted the bullets, took care of us, gave us treatment and then put us back against the wall and turned the guns on us once again.

The following morning, accompanied by Sergeant Bellosguardo, we turned up at the exit gate where there were both Italian and German guards on duty. Each of the two of us had a light bag. We handed over the documents and the passes. Our guard scarcely gave them a glance before giving the two sheets of paper to his German colleague. At that moment, a car horn started hooting violently: the car belonged to the Komandant, who wanted out. The German guard needed his hands free of the documents, so he handed them back to our duty officer, and rushed to open the gates. The sergeant gave the documents back to us and ran to give him a hand. Bellosguardo pushed us bodily away from the checkpoint. Proceeding like two stupefied robots, we walked on I don't know for how long, holding the passes tightly between our fingers. When the station was in sight, we were able to relax and look each other in the face. We burst into loud, liberating laughter, exclaiming at the same time: 'My God, talk about brass neck!'

Then we started to run. It seemed as though we were in a sequence of a comic film by Max Linder: there were never any dead moments. Everything went hell for leather, without a pause. We arrived at the platform, the train for Milan was standing there, we got on and it set off. There was a great crush of passengers, but we found two seats next to two girls who immediately smiled at us as though we were a pair of dandies on holiday instead of a couple of scruffy simpletons. A conversation was struck up, we offered them cigarettes, they took out of their bag a loaf of bread made with flour so dark it looked like rye, and offered us a piece each.

At the Sesto San Giovanni station, we had to change train. There was half an hour to wait. 'Listen, Marco, I'll go and post our letters to the Tradate headquarters.'

'Oh yes, our requests to enlist . . . they had completely slipped my mind!'

The post boxes were outside the station, on the other side of the piazza. I went out . . . crossed over . . . in the middle of the piazza I bumped into a crowd of people. There, in an avenue of plane trees, they were gathered in a circle around a man lying full length on a small grassy patch. He had a sign on his chest: 'Bandit'. I asked for information and a woman in tears replied: 'They killed him half an hour ago. They said they surprised him as he was distributing subversive leaflets.'

Someone else added: 'It seems he was a worker from Breda, a partisan.' I stood there petrified, observing that dead man with his arms outstretched. His mouth was open as though he were about to cry out.

'Move, move. On your way!' A group of the Black Brigades pushed us away from the avenue. I made my way back to the station, sick at heart, my face grey. I found Marco. It took a terrible effort to tell him about the shot partisan. I could not do it. I had continual bouts of vomiting.

Early in the afternoon, we arrived at Tradate. We went up to the castle where both the squadron HQ and the training school were billeted. We handed over our documents to a young officer, who ushered us into a large room.

'Come forward,' we were ordered by a medical officer behind a desk, 'take off your rags and throw them on that bench.' I found it hard to move: I was still stunned and could not get the image of that appalling act of violence out of my mind. We stood to attention, totally naked, in front of the desk.

'You're a disgrace!' exclaimed the paratroopers' medic. 'OK, the final debacle is at hand, but derelicts of this sort have never crossed my path before.' End of the comic film. The grotesque, with sniggers, was about to begin.

'Sorry, boys, I didn't want to mortify you, but stand in front of that mirror.' He pointed to a big, opaque sheet of glass which still contained the remnants of the decor of a piece of antique furniture: our reflections appeared as though reproduced through a cloud of steam. We did not make an edifying spectacle. 'Where have you come from?' As he spoke, he was leafing through the documents the sergeant had handed him.

'We're from the barracks at Monza, well, first we were at Mestre,' we started, breaking in to give each other a hand. 'We got caught up in a blitz, we ended up eating like dogs and both of us caught dysentery. Twice we came close to being dispatched to Germany . . . in four months we lost as much weight as if they had given us three tapeworms and oysters to swallow every day!'

The medical officer laughed: 'Well, at least you've not lost your sense of humour. Put your underpants, trousers and all the rest back on. You can go, there's no point in going on with the examination. You are not suitable.'

'What!' we stuttered.

'I'm sorry. I like you but you are too thin and underweight. This is a heavy course. It would knock out even an athlete from the Gallarate Sports Club.'

'But we used to go to the Gallarate Sports Club!'

'You? Are you making a fool of me?'

'Not at all. Until a couple of weeks ago, we were training with Missoni in the four hundred metres. We've raced with Siddi and Paternini.' The medical officer whispered into his assistant's ear something which sent him speeding out of the room. Then he got to his feet and came over to us, and almost mockingly felt our biceps, pectoral muscles, calves and buttocks.

'Yes, well, not too bad as regards toning, enough to make Volta's breast-stroke squad envious. To get you into minimum shape, you'd need to undergo fattening-up therapy, maybe with force-feeding through a tube, the way they do with the *paté de foie gras* geese. But we'll soon see if you're a couple of chancers or champions down on their luck!'

There was a knock at the door, and a muscular youth in shorts came in: 'Here I am!'

'Let me introduce you to the high-jump champion from the Gallarate Sports Club. Sergeant, cast you eye over these two. You recognise them?'

I try to turn towards the newcomer. They stop me. 'No, who are they?'

The medical officer points his finger at us: 'Enough of this shit, pair of bloody shysters!' The assistant is about to take us out, when I shout out: 'Enrico! Bloody hell, do you really not recognise me? It's Dario, from Porto Valtravaglia ... four hundred metres sprint.'

Enrico is thrown for a moment, he looks at us with a little more attention. Then he points to my comrade in misfortune: 'And you're Bianchi. Yes, now I remember. My God, you're all skin and bone. What's happened to you?'

'All right, all right,' the medical officer cuts us short. 'Keep the hugs and pleasantries for a later date. Get your kit off once again, you two, and we'll complete the examination.' End of Round 1.

Now it is time for the grand finale: test of courage and aptitude. They escorted us over to a field behind the castle where there stood a large, iron trellis-work tower, over fifteen metres high.

'Come on,' Enrico Ferri encouraged us, 'climb up.'

'Right up to the top?' we asked, our hearts in our mouths.

'That's right, then you've got to jump off.'

'Onto a safety net, I hope.'

'No, using a brake rope.'

'What's that?'

'The corporal on the platform at the top will explain everything.'

'Could we not have a little hint?'

'Shut up and get climbing.'

'How do you get up? Where's the ladder?'

'There is no ladder, only alternating grips in the main column. Look, it's easy, all you have to do is take hold of them one after the other and place your feet on the ones lower down. It's all a question of rhythm and arm strength.'

Off we go. We are already a few metres off the ground.

'The main thing,' Enrico Ferri shouted up to us, 'is to stay calm and relaxed as you get higher, and never look down, especially if you're prone to giddiness. Everything'd go haywire, and you'd plunge straight down.'

I take deep breaths, hold on, support myself on one leg . . . then pull up the other one. I clench my teeth, stretch out one arm and cling on. I'm at the seven-metre point: I feel numb, as though it were the first time I'd done any climbing. But for God's bloody sake, this is the same person who as a boy had gone hurtling down a mountainside hanging on to a cable wire, the same one who had plunged into the water from high up a cliffside! Yes, OK, but that was fool's courage! Now that I've reached the age of reason, I'm shitting myself with terror! Come on, another five metres, another seven grips, four, three, two . . . made it. Here I am on the platform. The corporal instructor drags me to my feet. I'm soaking with sweat. Bianchi makes it as well, as white as a sheet.

'Get your breath back, but move your arms about,' advises the instructor, 'and do some half-turns with your chest, otherwise you'll catch a chill. That's the idea, keep going. Meanwhile I'll tell you what's going to happen. Look up, and above your heads you'll see a pulley.' And he showed us a long pipe rotating on an iron axle. 'There's a rope tied around the pulley, with the other end attached to these harnesses which I'm going to ask you to put on, obviously one each. Be careful, the rotator is fixed onto one extremity of the axle. Take note: it's good and big, with four blades which rotate as they are pulled by the cable and dragged by your weight in descent, and so they brake the speed of the fall. You understand how it works?'

'And we've got to jump off just like that? Without a trial?'

'Exactly. This is the trial.'

'But is there anyone who's going to show us what to do . . . how it works?'

'No, that's why this is called the courage and aptitude test. If you are not up to it, it means that you're not suited for this discipline.'

In a flash, I saw the German guards sneering as they welcomed us back, arms outstretched. 'OK, I'll jump.'

The corporal checked the attachments of my harness. 'Right, you're all ready!' he said as he took me over to the edge of the platform. 'You've got to let yourself topple forward with your whole body almost rigid, then once you've jumped, open out your arms and hold your head up. When you're about to hit the ground, make your leg muscles go taut and bend your knees slightly. The moment you feel the impact, react as though you were about to jump up in the air. That's all there is to it. Take a deep breath and away you go!' A dozen or so recruits who had done the jump had gathered at the foot. They shouted with one voice: 'Don't be afraid! The fall velocity is only thirty kilometres an hour!' Then one of them with a baritone voice chimed in with the final message: 'I warn you, if your legs fold up like an accordion, you're done for! They don't take on dwarves here!'

General guffaw and I let myself fall forward as per the handbook. There was not even time to draw breath before I hit the ground. God, what a bump! I reacted awkwardly on landing, and nearly ended up on my back. They removed my harness. Marco came down as well. God help us, he came down at lightning speed, but he managed the final leap upwards better than me. We both received hefty slaps on the back from the medical officer. 'Well done, you've made it, you're enrolled!' Another flashback: the German guards reappear, this time cursing and swearing in disappointment.

At seven o'clock the following morning, we were lined up in the camp in squads of twenty each, around a hundred recruits in total, under the command of five instructors answerable to the captain of the training school. We began with warm-up exercises, the very same as we had done at the Gallarate club: bend to touch the toes, arm and leg stretching, short sprints, half-turns of chest and shoulders, press-ups, and so on, all executed at top speed, to the very limit of physical endurance. Half of the pupils were out of training, and in fact we all dropped one after the other, like skittles. Half an hour to get your breath back, then start all over again. In the afternoon, they gave out harnesses for us to put on, and then they suspended us from high bars held up by a structure similar to a swing: they invited us to swing about a bit, then without warning they sprang the catches supporting us and we found ourselves abruptly tossed to the ground: rolls and bumps at our own discretion. At this point, we embarked on lessons on the impact of landing, that is, they taught us somersault techniques. We had to learn how to carry out circular pirouettes while rolling on arms, shoulders, back and legs: how to transform ourselves into perfect wheels, with a suppleness which would enable us to adapt our rolling movement to any terrain or direction of impact. Of course they also taught us the angel drop with backward flip of the arms, and other acrobatic turns. As regards training for the jump itself, every day they taught us something new: diving jump into a tarpaulin, jump with weapons and rucksack, and finally the blind jump, that is, blindfolded, letting go of the swing while it was swaying. Obviously, sprains, dislocated joints and broken bones were the order of the day. And the instructors' refrain was always the same: 'Anyone who can't stand it can pack up this very moment!'

In the evening, we would be full of aches and pains, as well as worn out by sheer fatigue. Only a few had the energy to ask for an evening pass: the bulk of us lay on the camp beds chatting. As confidence among us grew, I grasped that others among the trainees felt the same way as me: we were taking part in that gut-bursting tour de force only to escape from something worse, but no one wanted to admit it explicitly. There were also some fanatical followers of the regime who came out with high-minded banalities about fatherland, sacrifice and defence of the race, but the majority ignored them. A large number of the lads had signed up for the course principally to prove to themselves that they had the necessary courage and physical strength, or else to escape from the shell of what they themselves considered a mediocre existence, bereft of all vitality. The commanders at the barracks at Monza had found out that we had skipped off to Tradate, but no one could ask for us to be sent back. In fact, it was as if we were in the Foreign Legion.

The forty days' training passed at incredible speed. We awaited the day of the jump with anxiety and trepidation, but unexpectedly the captain informed us that there were no aircraft available at the Venegono airfield. Some of the boys burst out crying in despair. There were only a few more days, then we were to be sent who knows where, perhaps to the front, perhaps to take part in a search-and-destroy mission near Cirié, in Piedmont. That very evening, Marco and I made up our minds it was time to get moving immediately. Taking advantage of an evening off, we ran to the station and got on the last train bound for the lake and along its shoreline. I had forged two other false passes. When we got to Laveno, we said goodbye. We had no precise programme for our escape. For the moment, Marco decided to go back to his family at Besozzo, then he would see. I got off at Porto Valtravaglia.

I found the whole family at home, and explained my situation to them. I was once again a deserter, but this time the stakes were higher. My father had a friend who lived at Caldé, a colleague with whom he had organised the escape of many wanted people. He already had an understanding with him: the railwayman would put me up in the attic of an old, semi-abandoned house which belonged to him. Half ruined and almost completely overgrown, it was situated in the woods in the depths of the valley. The attic could be reached only by a ladder; once I was inside, I was to pull it up and conceal it. No one, not even my mother, knew about that hiding place. In the attic, I found a straw bed and a cupboard with some provisions obtained by the railwayman. My father and his friend did not even say goodbye; a few waves and they were off. That night, I did not sleep a wink. Sounds and noises from the woods and surrounding fields filled my ears. There were no windows, only a skylight camouflaged by creepers, but I looked out through a hole in the tiles and in the distance I could see the lake. It was a moonlit night, and the noise of barking dogs was redoubled by the echo from the valleys.

Alba, the sister of the railwayman friend, was supposed to come within three days with fresh supplies, but no one turned up. On the evening of the fourth day, I heard the sound of the engine of a truck. I looked out of the usual peep-hole: it was a National Republican Guard patrol. They stopped right under the ruin. They were chatting, but I could not make out what they were saying. On the other side of the roof, beside the skylight, I had a rope in readiness as an alternative possible escape route, but I did not move. I was afraid to make any noise. I lay there, almost without breathing. Suddenly, the four or five of them climbed back into their truck and went away. I will never know why they were up there. Had someone been spying on me? Were they looking for someone else?

Alba, the Italian for Dawn, lived up to her name: she turned up exactly as dawn was breaking, three days late. She had with her a bag filled with foodstuffs. At long last! I had not so much as a jug of water left, but I did not dare go down. I was literally in a state of panic. The woman climbed up the ladders I let down to her. She apologised for the delay, but her brother had had to flee at short notice. The Blackshirts were after him, and so she too had had to stay in hiding.

I spent more than a month up there, without ever going out. From my vantage point, I was able to spy all around. I learned to decipher the greater part of the noises and rustles of the woodland; I came to recognise the song of the various birds, the subtle calls of each animal, the porcupines, ferrets, mice, otters, beech marten and foxes. They were my guard: it was they who gave the alarm or fell instantly silent if someone seemed to be drawing close to our territory. In my turn, I had become part of the fauna of the locality; they knew who I was, and above all knew I was inoffensive. I often threw them handfuls of crumbs, the remains of my meals. Some birds even came up to my peep-hole. Every so often I climbed up to look out through the skylight. It was possible to make out some peasant houses in the valley on the far side of the woods. Who knows if under those roofs there were other fugitives hidden in the same conditions as me.

I believe it was a Tuesday, there was a really bright sun, and all over the valley, as far as the eye could see, the flowers were in bloom. I heard blasts in the distance, and bells began to ring out one after the other from all the bell-towers in the neigh-bourhood. The wind was in my favour, and even the sound of bells on the far side of the lake carried over to me. I crawled through the skylight, and climbed out onto the roof from where I could see the piazza in Caldé. There was a band playing their hearts out, and young men, women and children were running about all over the place. They were yelling, but I could not make out a word. I did hear the festive shouts of people making their way up to the ruined house. I immediately recog-nised Alba, her friends, the railwayman and other inhabitants of the valley. 'It's all over!' they kept on repeating in a loud voice, 'The war is over!'

# CHAPTER 25

## *Revisiting Grandfather Bristin*

Now that the war was over, Porto Valtravaglia went through a period of wild euphoria. Professor Civolla kept repeating: 'What we finally have before us is an enormous blank page on which to write new ideas and new dreams!' I started travelling with Bianca and Fulvio back and forth to Milan, but I spent more and more time in the city near Largo La Foppa, where my mother had rented a little villa, the property of the railway company.

One Saturday in May, I went to visit my grandfather, whom I had not seen for almost a year. Nino, one of my uncles, offered to take me in his car, known as the 'hotchpotch', so called because it had been put together with bits and pieces from various cars and from scrap recovered from the foundry. 'Thank you, I'll be glad to come along . . . and let's hope that we make it as far as Sartirana!' The journey was a bit of an adventure. We had to get a horse to pull the car across the Po. When we got near Grandfather's farm, my uncle parked his jalopy in a neighbour's stable, begging him not to breathe a word to his father about that collection of scrap metal: Bristìn would have skinned him alive with his mockery.

We found Granddad in the middle of his farmyard, putting the final touches to a 'conservatory'. It had an enormous conical-shaped cupola of a roof, at least ten metres high, whose base rested directly on the ground. The cone covered a large well, at least ten metres in diameter and the same in depth. The conical cupola was made of interwoven wood and reeds, so that it looked like a big, upturned basket. Entry to the well was via a spiral staircase dug into the ground and reinforced with planks and boards of alder wood, and at the bottom there was a press of snow and ice from the winter cold. The plan was to preserve dairy produce, meat, vegetables and even fish on that deep frozen base. In short, it was the kind of refrigerator in use among the Romans: a 'conservatory', in other words. Grandfather's eyesight had deteriorated considerably in recent times, and to oversee that kind of temple, he needed the help of the eldest of his sons, Aronne. I was deeply moved as I embraced him, and as he gave me a kiss I felt his cheeks were damp.

The following day was a Sunday, when no work is done in the fields, so I convinced him to pose for me for a portrait. He had on a velvet jacket and a newly ironed shirt, and sat bolt upright as though he were on horseback. I needed him to relax and not to appear to be encased in plaster, so to put him at ease I threw at him a load of questions on problems which I knew were close to his heart.

'Excuse me, Granddad, but what's happening now to your orchards, trees and greenhouses? Who's left to help you?'

'No one. Who do you think is interested in this work? I've got five sons and three daughters, and I was the first, even if involuntarily, to do everything to make sure they had other interests. I got them passionately interested in mechanics by dragging every kind of machine, even an electric-powered pump, into the house! I taught them how to dismantle and reassemble engines, driving them crazy by making them do it over and over again. A peasant cannot only know about sowing

and harvesting, spreading shit . . . I beg your pardon, manure
and verdigris on the vines. If he limits himself to that, he will
never be anything more than a country bumpkin, with all the
vision of a blinkered horse. Be curious, throw open all the
windows of your brain! And they have thrown them open.
Beniamino has become a test pilot with Macchi in Varese,
Giosuè is an insurance agent, Mattia is a gold engraver in
Valence, and Nino, as you know, is also mad about engines. He
has taken a diploma in mechanical engineering and now he's
enrolled for an evening course at the *politecnico* in Milan.
Aronne, the only one who gave me a hand with the farm work,
has gone and decided to set up a garage. I have chased my sons
off the land! But don't worry, I have no intention of letting my
barns go to wrack and ruin. I'm putting together a cooperative
of young people just back from the war. I'm very gradually
getting them broken in. It was them you saw yesterday, putting
up the cupola-conservatory. They're coming along nicely.
I make them pay a little rent, and if it all works out, I'll hand
the lot over to them.'

Grandfather was beginning to relax. He was throwing his
arms about and gesticulating, and at one point even got to his
feet.

'Hey, Granddad, where are you going? I'm doing your
portrait.'

'Ah, yes, sorry.' He came round behind me to get a better
look at the painting. 'Goodness! Wait till I change glasses. Well
done, that's me exactly!' He gave me a slap on the back and
went back to his seat. Now he was silent, following his own
thoughts, then, as though talking to himself, he came out with:
'And to think that I was born a *perdapé*.'

'*Perdapé*? What does that mean, Granddad?'

'It's the bottom level, the lowest rank among peasants. They are the tenant farmers who have the right to take what remains of the crops only after the landlord has taken his fixed share. And if the harvest goes badly that year, they die. The *perdapé* contract is called the *angheria*, in other words the 'vexation'. Does that term not say something to you? Look at it, I was born to *perdere i piedi*, to lose my feet, destined to wear out my feet by having them sunk in the earth from dawn to dusk.'

When winter was over, I went back to visit my grandfather. I met him coming towards me as I came out of the station, using his stick to pick his way among the trunks of the lime trees on either side of him in the avenue. The people he met called out to him, said hello, stopped to chat and tried to needle Bristìn into coming out with one of his witty, trenchant remarks. He was by now almost completely blind, but he put up with this situation with an impressive degree of self-irony. Occasionally he would walk backwards: 'In this way,' he explained to those who questioned him about this odd habit, 'I manage to get the sun on my face, and that gives me great pleasure. And anyway, what's the point of walking forwards? I can't see a thing!'

When he was at home, he was never on his own. Peasants came to ask his advice about planting such-and-such citrus fruits or cereals, to check whether the moon was right, or if the seeds they had bought at the cooperative were any good. It was true that he could not see but, as he had taught me as a boy, touch and smell were infallible tools of judgement. He would plunge his hand into the sack of grain or rice, let the seeds run through his fingers as though they were rosary beads, then he would sniff at them, put them in his mouth and chew them. At the end he gave his verdict. Bristìn was the terror of seed merchants.

Many times he insulted his peasant friends who came along to show him the anti-cryptogamic concoctions the consortium had advised them to use to get rid of moths, mole crickets and other scourges of the fields: 'It's quite true, bonehead, that with these pesticides you can wipe out at least ten bastard variations of seed-devourer, but have you ever thought of how many other grubs of good insects you would slaughter? No, you didn't, did you? Take DDT, for instance, look at the damned disaster that brought . . . last year, you remember, they flew over the fields with an aeroplane spraying out this poisonous sludge as though it were holy water at Corpus Christi. "It is a panacea, a marvel," intoned the agronomists . . . the bastards, as ignorant as pigshit they were. Oh yes, it's true, they did away with the bugs in the maize, the weeds in the rice-fields . . . there were savings on rice-weeders, red mushrooms and phylloxera. But at the same time, they killed nesting birds, fireflies, bees, dragonflies, frogs, carps by the ton, and even flocks of swallows. What a bunch of swine! You eliminate the birds, sparrows and starlings, you kill off the blackbirds . . . and then you're surprised that processionary caterpillars grow tenfold and strip bare whole woods of poplars, tearing them apart. But who was it – you tell me, hare-brain – who was it who in years past used to gobble all those thousand-footed, slimey grubs when they dangled from branches, hanging from their own slobber like so many miniature Tarzans? The swallows, sparrows, starlings and so on! And it was the same with the frogs: it was they that swallowed the larvae of the mosquitoes and horseflies as they floated on the waterways. It was the dragonflies who got rid of the vermin which devour the rye and the tender potato flower. Now it will take years before that astonishing equilibrium can be re-established!'

'So are you saying that we should stop praying weed-killers and pesticides . . . should we stand by and watch these vermin destroy our crops?'

'For God's sake, no. Chemistry and progress are sacred things, but don't trust anybody straight off, as though you were blind moles: get the information! Stop holding on to the damn idea that all that's important is to secure your own advantage, and the hell with whatever comes after. Look, it's like hitting out when you're playing *lippa*, the kind of rounders game they play in these parts. You strike, the *lippa* flies through the air but there's always the risk it will come down slap-bang in somebody's eye. Sure, not everything that brings death is necessarily negative. My grandmother treated her sciatica by having herself bitten on the buttocks by a poisonous snake, and incredibly enough she was completely cured. But her sister was stung by a wasp and died. In nature, everything can be overturned, everything has its double, negative or positive. You can never say: "I do not know the effect of this medicine, nor do I want to know." No, you've got to know, you've got to get the information, you've got to learn; otherwise, this great mother Nature will become as ferocious and vindictive as an ordinary god, and strangle us all in our cradles . . . or will poison us while she breast-feeds us at her great tits!'

I stood close by, listening, always fascinated by how my grandfather managed to express such important concepts with such simplicity. As I observed his gestures, I imprinted each lesson of his in my brain, and there came to my mind that stupendous maxim by Montesquieu: 'An erudite expert is one who uses complex terms and expressions to communicate nothing at all.' My grandfather was exactly the opposite.

The former students of the Faculty of Agrarian Studies, all now graduated and well advanced in the practice of their profession, often came to visit him. Punctually, every Friday, he received a visit from the parish priest of Torreberetti. He and the priest would take a seat in the wisteria bower, and their conversation was never less than animated. Once I heard my grandfather roar: 'The fact is that if you are to survive, my dear Roman and Apostolic Catholics, you need all the rites of holy religion, starting with confession which frees you of all guilt: a touch of repentance and you're on your way again. If you've got problems, you get down on your knees and say a prayer to Our Lord, the saints, or Our Lady to come and fix things up for you. We atheists, on the other hand, have no saint to attach ourselves to. For our guilt, we can only turn to our consciences. If we've got problems, we've only got our reason to rely on!'

Soon after, as he was waving goodbye to the parish priest, who was now in the distance, he commented: 'I'll have to watch out I don't go too far with him. What's going to happen is that one fine day he'll start having doubts, pull off his vestments and turn atheist. Then I'll have to go and take his place in the parish.'

Three years later, my grandfather died. There was a huge crowd at his funeral, many from the farms round about. Some came from the other side of the River Po. They were all on bicycles. Since the Sartirana cemetery was on the other side of the railway line and the canal, they followed the hearse, as was the custom with every funeral, cycling slowly. It was not considered respectful to follow by motorbike. A procession with so many bicycles swarming silently over the plain was, to say the least, a bit surreal!

I pedalled close to the Torreberetti priest, who was not wearing clerical garb. The professor from Alessandria had been asked to say a few words of farewell at the grave-side.

One sentence has remained alive in my memory: 'At the death of a peasant who knew his own land and who knew the history of the men who worked that land, at the death of a wise man who knew how to read the moon and sun, the winds and the flight of the birds, as Bristìn did, it is not only one man who dies: it is a whole library which is burned down.'

## CHAPTER 26

## *Waiting for Picasso*

I was in my second year at the Brera Academy and had chosen the course on frescos with Achille Funi, an extraordinary teacher. Every so often, Carrà, a highly likable as well as talented man, would take the class. In the post-war period, all the academic conventions and rules had been set aside: any student was free to go to any class and follow an entire lesson without fear of being asked to leave. So it was that every so often I would turn up in the principal lecture hall where the sculpture instructor was Marino Marini. On another occasion, I managed to get into the studio of Giacomo Manzoni, better known as Manzù, to fashion clay on the lathe, to help in the operations of casting plaster and fusing moulds. There was no timetable: it was permitted to carry on working even after six o'clock in the evening . . . not in all classrooms, obviously. In Perspective, that is in the School of Stage Design, it was possible to enter even after dinner, right up until night-time. The director of this genuinely free academy was Aldo Carpi, recently returned in poor physical condition from the Matthausen labour camp. He had always shown himself to be a man of extraordinary cultural and civil openness, a true example of what is meant by 'free ideas'.

My companions at the academy included Morlotti, Peverelli, Alik Cavaliere, Bobo Piccoli, Parzini, all of whom would make a certain name for themselves in succeeding years. I was not aware of it, but I was living in a really extra-ordinary and unrepeatable moment of our history, from both the political and cultural point of view. Among the *trattorias* and *osterias* of Via Fiori Chiari and Via Fiori Scuri, inter-spersed with the occasional brothel, there were colourful shops and bars like the *Jamaica* and *Le Sorelle Pirovini*. At any moment you could run into people of great importance: writers, theatre and cinema directors who later became famous. I often found myself seated at the same table as them in the Fiori Chiari, eating plates of badly cooked and badly flavoured pasta. But nobody minded. The only complainants were our stomachs.

We talked about everything, about the political situation, about stage sets, about the Italian and foreign books which we were finally able to read after twenty years of Fascist censor-ship. We did not have much money, often we had to tighten our belts or live on what we could borrow, but I have never lived in such a climate of carefree rumbustiousness as in those days and at that level.

Often, while we were in the Jamaica having a sandwich, my friends would encourage me to tell them some new tale, and there was no escape, even when I was not in the mood. By now I had put together a considerable repertoire, mainly of pieces with some reference to current affairs, but also of caricatures of our professors and great teachers whose mythical obses-sions, generosity and meanness were well known to us. One of the most frequently requested satires was on Carrà. I invited them to imagine the Master intent on painting one of his famous beaches with its brightly coloured cabins, and in the background the sea and a bather running along the water-line pursued by a playful dog jumping in the air. Carrà scratches the figure of the dog off the canvas three times: he cannot get it right. Finally he asks his wife to act as model: 'Get into the right pose, on all fours, please . . . that's it . . . just like that . . . now make a gesture of leaping . . . try harder . . . paws up . . . yelp a little. Pity you don't have a tail.' Obviously, in this case, the situation was ironical and had little to do with reality, unlike in others, such as the one which satirised the behaviour of De Chirico. The most requested sketch was the one in which I performed dialogues between various characters, the merchant who begs the Master to reproduce his most famous masterpieces from his metaphysical period. De Chirico fends him off, but sets to work with the help of a pupil once he has fixed the price. Here was the Master of metaphysics seized by a creative impulse, painting at top speed and reproducing the same subject on four different canvases. As though he were on an assembly line, he is overwhelmed by his own demonic rhythm and slaps paint over the pupil and the merchant who is standing by, desperate for the 'merchandise'. At this point, as he evaluates the result, the Master decides to introduce into the four copies some variants on the original, the famous piazza in Ferrara with the castle, the towers and the height-ened perspective sloping down to the sea. 'Here we are, I'll add an extra tower, and instead of the grey sea, I'll put in a nice green, stormy sea. I could trick this one out with some little pyramids in the background and a yacht out at sea. On this one, I could do a female nude: *Dido Abandoned*. On the sea, we could have a ship sinking beneath the waves.' The whole thing, obviously, recounted with mime gestures to suggest the frenzy of his painting.

Everything is ready.

But having several times altered the sequence of his paintings, the Master can no longer remember which is the original, particularly since, in the confusion, he has painted over it as well. Finally, he piles up the paintings one on top of the other as though they were a pack of cards, and gets his dog, obviously blindfolded, to pull it out of the pack with his teeth.

But I did not always perform on my own. Often Emilio Tadini came to my aid and took over with his splendid repertoire of old Neapolitan numbers, accompanying himself on the guitar. Then Busnelli, a born acrobat, would execute on the spot, in the middle of the street, his own incredible series of cartwheels. But the greatest fun we had came from the big practical jokes we devised, like the one we set up to celebrate Pablo Picasso and his first visit to Milan. An extraordinary affair!

A group including Morlotti, Peverelli and others had managed to arrange a meeting with the great Master in his atelier in Paris. Picasso greeted them with great cordiality. It was known that the Galleria Manzoni in Milan was about to reopen with an exhibition of many works by the Spanish Master. When invited to come to Milan for the inauguration, Picasso had replied: 'I might be able to manage, but I can't give any guarantees.'

A few journalists, desperate for a scoop at any cost, got to know about the conversation in Paris, and quite calmly wrote that Picasso's arrival in Milan for the opening could be regarded as a done deal.

Other newspapers picked up the story, which was then broadcast on the radio. We, in our turn, decided to do our bit for the supreme artist: 'We'll see to it that he really does come. Picasso will be in Milan in flesh and blood.'

The cornerstone of our project was Otello, the janitor at the Brianza, who helped out with casting operations in Marino Marini's studio. Around fifty years old, squat in stature, robust in build, skull embellished with stray wisps of white hair and face identical to that of the leader of the Cubist school. In other words, the spitting image of Picasso.

It was decided. We coaxed the janitor to join our game. By the purest good fortune, Otello had worked for ten years in Marseilles and spoke near-perfect French. Picasso is to arrive on the 11.30 Paris-Milan express. We spread the news through the agencies and gave it directly to the radio and newspapers. We got hold of a white trench coat and made our janitor put it on. We turned up at the Stazione Garibaldi a good hour early and made him, accompanied by Alix Cavaliere, Morlotti and Bobo Picccoli, get on the train for Gallarate. At the station at Rho, they got off and waited for the train from Menton, which was due to stop, as it always does, at that junction of the four lines.

At the Central Station in Milan, platform ten, there was a great crowd: journalists, photographers, newsreel cameramen, students, artists and intellectuals. There was even one red flag.

The train drew in and the crowd surged forward to greet the artist.

'Do you think he'll be in the first coach or nearer the back?'

The passengers got off.

'Did you catch sight of Picasso in one of the carriages?'

The train was emptying. No sign of Picasso.

'There he is!'

Yes, it was him all right. He leaned out of a window, gave a wave then disappeared and got off at the platform opposite. 'He's an original, eh!'

People climbed aboard to get off on the other side. He'd vanished.

'He must have slipped into an underground passage.'

The photographers and journalists gave chase. A voice called out. 'Take it easy, he's not run away. It's just that the sight of a crowd makes him panic. If you want to meet him, come along this evening to the rooms of the *Filodrammatici* theatre company, beside La Scala. There'll certainly be refreshments as well as a more relaxed press conference which promises to be historic.'

The *Filodrammatici* space was a kind of hangar used as a rehearsal room. They were restoring it, so it was crammed with scaffolding and planks under a pseudo art nouveau style cupola, but the iron structures were also ideal for hanging the back-cloths of a stage set. For this purpose, we had enrolled stage-design students and a couple of set designers from the *Piccolo Teatro*. They had procured some unneeded materials from past productions: a couple of papier maché statues, a dragon and rearing horse, all on wheels. The first to turn up that evening were the musicians from Santa Tecla, who took up their position on a raised platform while the lights were still being put in place. Not long after, a group of girls from the *Scuola Lambro Dance* made their appearance, prancing about and trying out the parquet flooring with their footwork.

Finally, people started to arrive. We were busy putting out the seats in a truly chaotic order. The Santa Tecla band struck up a well-known piece – *All God's Children Gotta Shoes*.

There were more people than we had expected, including some very well turned-out ladies. Many of them had plainly deserted the first night at the opera. Schwarz, the king of art dealers, was there with his whole court. The audience was not quite seated before the first of the comic turns took place: up above, clinging onto the scaffolding, a painter in a white overall started screaming for help. It was Busnelli doing a bit of clowning: he let himself slide down a wire, then began to sway wildly backwards and forwards. He's falling! No, he's clutching a plank. Some firemen, among whom I made out some young actors from the *Fantasio Piccoli* troupe, clambered up a ladder. They told the audience to stand close to the walls: 'It's dangerous,' they shout, 'clear the centre of the hall.' In fact one set of ladders did fall, yet miraculously did not crash to the ground but remained dangling from a rope. The rearing horse on wheels came careering towards the audience, followed by the dragon spinning on itself. The carousel created havoc and some of the ladies uttered shrill screams which tuned in perfectly with the jangle of sounds coming from the orchestra's saxophones and trumpets.

One of the guests, jumping out of the dragon's way, asked in a loud voice: 'When is Picasso coming?'

'Relax! He'll be here any moment.'

A siren was heard and a door was flung open: from the far end of the hall, a policeman on his motor-bicycle made his entrance and asked for silence: 'What is this madhouse? Have we all gone off our heads? Do you have permission for this show? Who is the director, the producer? Can you tell me what you're doing here?'

'We're waiting for Pablo Picasso.'

'Pablo's coming here?' whinnied the motorcycle policeman. He let out a scream, revved up his bike, then sped off at top speed, nearly knocking over the dancing girls, who leapt into the arms of the firemen-clowns.

The orchestra was getting more and more frenzied. Five painters and decorators entered and made out that they were there to get on with the work. I was one of these clown-painters. We dragged in an enormous canvas, the kind used to throw over furniture to protect it from dripping paint, and forced the audience to file under it. Two elderly ladies asked loudly: 'But when is Picasso due?'

'He's coming, he's coming.'

Meantime, the decorators had taken to throwing buckets at each other, soaking themselves with lashings of paint (of course, it was the usual coloured soap). A large part of the audience now got the joke and joined in: many girls grabbed hold of the canvas covering and started shaking it about. No one paid any heed to the splashes of the painted soap any longer, apart from some ladies who lamented: 'Oh no! That's enough of this paint. When's Picasso going to arrive?'

'He's coming, he's coming.'

The orchestra struck up a triumphal march, the trumpets blared out a thunderous entrance tune worthy of a circus, and fireworks went off.

'Right, Picasso's finally arrived!'

And there he was. Through the smoke and bangs, the profile of Otello, still in his white trench coat, could be made out.

Applause.

'It really is him!'

Otello was about to speak: '*Mes amis, je suis ravi d'être ici . . .*'

One of the firemen-clowns was holding on to a large water

pipe, which split apart. Disaster! A jet of water of apocalyptic proportions poured down on us. We were all soaked.

Picasso yelled out: 'Ah no, fuck it!'

Rush for the exits . . . some oaths, but much laughter. A splendid, very wet lady, who seemed to be emerging from the waves after a shipwreck, appeared contented enough but was heard to make the comment: 'I'll remember this occasion as long as I live. But was that really Picasso?'

# CHAPTER 27

## In Paris

Each one of us in the Brera dreamed of making his own journey to Paris, the capital of modern art. Paris was for us what the Holy Land had been for Christians in the Middle Ages. It was the Mecca of every apprentice artist, painter, writer or poet. I, too, dreamed of making that journey, and it was ironic how it happened. It all began with a commission which was, to put it mildly, unusual, not least in the workplace itself: the Monumental Cemetery in Milan. The job was to do a fresco on the inner and outer walls of a grave . . . yes, a grave, a tomb of imposing aspect. An architect friend had designed and built a chapel with octagonal base, copper dome and red porphyry columns, a kind of mausoleum for the members of a wealthy family from the Brianza . . . Brustello or Brustelli, I can't quite remember. The patrons were very pleased with their final residence, but they found the inside too bare: it was all white, a bit too sepulchral. 'I'm for something a bit more cheerful!' the most likely first guest of the mausoleum, the octogenarian pater familias, had insisted.

And so we, the band of the 'Painting of Cheerful Death with mosaic tesserae', were brought in. In a few weeks, we prepared the sketches for the fresco which was to take in all seven walls (the eighth was the entrance). The tombs themselves were to be under the floor. We took our inspiration from the mosaics of the Mausoleum of Galla Placidia in Ravenna, with its tracery of stylised vine shoots and labyrinths of geometrical shapes twined round each other. The dome was to be painted in light blue with a scattering of cirri and wispy clouds.

I have to be truthful: it got you down to be living for almost a month among graves. Above all, just as you were beginning to get engrossed in the work, you would hear outside chants and litanies from priests, clerics and nuns processing with that day's newly deceased. Since we were behind with the commission, we had to work late into the evening. When the custodian came along to get us out, it was already night. Walking back through votive lamps by the hundred, rows of praying angels, distraught female figures, male and female saints with outstretched arms induced us, as Italian superstition requires, to cheerfully touch the bobbly, decorative parts of the male reproductive system. Within three weeks, the job was done. Our clients were highly satisfied. 'Look, what a lovely little space it's turned out to be,' said the family's grande dame, 'I might get another one built exactly the same instead of the bower in the park, then I could sit there gossiping with my friends as we sip our tea.'

Now I had a fair sum of money, enough for my travel.

Emilio Tadini, who at that stage had not yet started painting but who was writing subtle, intense poetry, decided to come with me.

Travel by train, obviously. When we reached our destination, we scarcely took the time to drop off our bags at the hotel before we were out on the streets in search of the museums. By the end of the week, we were like two punch-drunk boxers: out of one gallery, into another!

In the evening, to draw breath, we went to the theatre, avant-garde comic theatre, such as *La Pomme Rouge* or *L'ane en Chaines*, a cabaret of dangerously *osé* satire. I remember one scene in which six splendid girls appeared and with great elegance began to strip until they were completely naked, or nearly so. They were about to remove their G-strings when – whoops! – six dicks complete with decorative little balls! As the spectators guffawed in somewhat dismayed, indeed disappointed, laughter, the striptease girls peered in astonishment at those little appendages which had so unexpectedly protruded, and squealed in falsetto tones as they fled from the stage.

I swear that neither Emilio nor I ever understood if those penises were fake, and if we were confronted with enchanting transvestites or even with a sextet of carefully selected hermaphrodites!

In the following number, another nude girl appeared, totally intent on removing body hair with wax and tweezers . . . each time she plucked hair off, she uttered groans and incomprehensible oaths. Then she started squeezing imperceptible blackheads, while at the same time confiding in us, as though we were in her room backstage, about intimate problems to do with her profession as a striptease artist. She complained of a wicked headache and was really annoyed at having to make a living by exciting dirty-minded spectators, especially those who could not even take the trouble to conceal their nasty hand manoeuvres during her number. As she spoke, she was rubbing cream over her belly and buttocks, checking the result in a mirror. She continued to give vent to her irritation over her emotional life: she had a fairly well-to-do lover, but he bored her. Another rub of the cream, this time on her breasts, with a special touch of bright red for her nipples. Then she confided in us about the great love of her life: a right bastard, currently in jail, who exploited her, beat her, then kissed her gently, so that they ended up making love. As she described to us, with the aid of mime, their love-making, she filed the hard skin on her heels.

Finally she drew back a curtain, behind which a toilet seat appeared. She sat down on it and did a pee . . . she sighed and sobbed. She pulled the chain, and switched off the light. End of sketch.

I am not going to tell you about all the other shows: that was only a sample.

I felt my brain battered this way and that, like a table-tennis ball: from Braque to Feydeau, from the Jeu de Paume with Manet to the Salle Gémier with the most recent play by Camus.

We two poor little provincials certainly did not succeed in taking in all those emotions at one go. In my own case, I could never have imagined that those places would become familiar to me some decades later. None more so that the mythical Salle Gémier, one of the most prestigious theatres in France.

It was there in 1973 that I made my début with *Mistero buffo*, my first live performance in Europe.

# CHAPTER 28

## My Father'S Funeral

My father died at the grand old age of ninety in the early months of 1987. He went quietly and serenely, almost unexpectedly, but he had made all the funeral arrangements in advance, starting with the band which he wanted to accompany his body to the cemetery in Luino. The conductor of the town's brass band was a long-standing friend of his. One evening some months previously, my father had paid him a visit to agree on the pieces to be performed. He even set about searching out and handing over the scores of the various marches he wanted played. His choice was a medley, rewritten in march time, of all the partisan songs from the valleys, including Ossola and the surrounding area, where the most bloody encounters with the Germans and the Fascist brigades had taken place. The first number on the programme was to be *Val Sesia,* a slow, dignified number, as powerful as the river which gave it its name. The next work was to be the march of the partisans from Val Comeggia, which was more like a dance-hall waltz than a patriotic anthem: then came the famous *Se non ci ammazza i crucchi, se non ci ammazza i bricchi* (If the Krauts Don't Kill Us, If the Peaks Don't Kill Us) from Val Vigezzo, and so on, right down to the inevitable *Bella Ciao,* and a closing rendering of *Addio Lugano bella.*

A half-hour before the stipulated time, the little piazza in the spur of land where the Fo family lived was jam-packed with people. There were trade unionists, socialists and communists with their banners, a group of relatives of the Jewish families my father had helped escape to the Canton Ticino, and finally a small delegation of anarchists. The railwaymen were the most numerous, but there were also border guards and, standing a little further off, representatives of the old smugglers from Pino. By the time the coffin was carried out of the house, people were crowded right up the streets around the piazza . . . more red banners seemed to be sprouting on every side.

We had to hurry things along: the road to the cemetery was quite long. The band took up its place at the head of the procession and struck up with *Val Sesia*. The coffin moved off, followed by all of us, sons, daughters and grandchildren, uncles and aunts, then banners and standards flying freely . . . a real forest of flags. No priests, no nuns. The band was already a kilometre off, and still the tail of the procession had not moved from the assembly point. There was no doubt that the majority of the inhabitants of Luino and the Valtravaglia were there.

We walked along the lakeside and reached the long curve which rises up towards the hill. Down below, perched on a granite cliff, stood the Romanesque church with its high steeple. At that moment, the band was playing the waltz-time march, and the procession seemed to lurch a little. Ahead, the musicians quickened their step and accompanied the *allegro con brio* tempo of the piece they were playing with a swing of the hips and a drop of the shoulders. Many people in the cortège had almost forgotten they were participating in a 'mournful ceremonial' and executed little dance-step hops and skips, but then they composed themselves once again.

I imagined my father peeping out from somewhere or other, enjoying himself and guffawing . . . happily. (After all, wasn't his name Felice, which means 'Happy'?)

We were crossing the piazza in front of the old town hall: the band moved on to *Bella ciao*, played at the tempo of a cross-country race. As the coffin-bearers speeded up, the whole cortège was forced to step it out more briskly. The skipping march would not do any more: we were now onto the rhythms of an infantry charge, with the attendant flurry of banners. Groups of curious onlookers lining the streets applauded and asked: 'What's the rush? Who are you going to bury?'

'A railwayman, and just for once he wants to be on time.'

We were now level with the Romanesque church: many people had gathered on the sloping piazza in front of the porch, but they had not come for my father's funeral. They were waiting for the hearse bearing the body of Piero Chiara, the famous author of satirical novels, all set in Luino itself. The body was to be brought from Varese where he had died, and it was late. But his crowd of mourners, seeing the arrival of an impressive cortège with a flutter of red flags and a scattering of anarchist banners, immediately exclaimed: 'Must be him! Obviously, an anti-cleric like him . . . you could hardly expect him to bring along a procession of priests and bishops. Red he lived, and red he died!'

And so it was that, without another word, they all climbed down the two staircases and lined up behind the multi-bannered crowd marching to the rhythm of a regimental band. Some of them began to sing quietly the opening words of the first verse:

*La mia mamma la mi diceva,*
*Non andare sulle montagne,*
*Mangerai sol polenta e castagne*
*Ti verrà l'acidità.*

My dear old mum, she used to say,
Stay clear of hills and mountains,
Polenta and chestnuts are very poor fare
And they're bad for your digestion!

Another three hundred metres and this sea of people reached the great arched entrance to the graveyard and began to file in. Meanwhile, down below, in front of the church, the hearse with the body of Piero Chiara arrived. There was no one waiting for it except the sacristan, who was almost helpless with laughter as he observed the scene: 'There were lots of people here, but they all went off to the funeral of Fo, the station master!'

The driver of the hearse and his followers caught up with the mourners for their deceased before they disappeared into the cemetery. 'Hey, you've got the wrong funeral: your coffin's here, on this hearse. Go back to the church!'

'Oh, what a muck-up! Right, new orders: everybody back down!'

About-turn, a few oaths, a lot of laughter. The people started running, waving arms and shouting, all to a march tempo:

*La mia morosa la mi diceva*
*Non andare coi ribelli.*
*Non avrai più i miei lunghi capelli*
*Sul cuscino a riposar!*

My darling love has said to me
Don't go to war to fight.
You'll no more play with my long hair
When you lie on my pillow at night!

If you think that this mad blunder, which looks as if it came from a farce, is the product of my wild imagination, all you have to do is get a hold of the *Corriere della Sera* for 4 January 1987. There you will find the report of this impossible adventure, whose staging is beyond all doubt to be attributed to the jovial ghost of my father, Felice.